# The Year I Fell Into  France

## My Recession-Proof Volunteer Journey

I0621294

# Mel Reyna Scott

Published by Melonie Scott Inc.

Published in the United States of America by Melonie Scott Inc.

ISBN (ebook): 979-8-9989633-0-8
ISBN (paperback): 979-8-9989633-1-5
ISBN (hardcover): 979-8-9989633-2-2
ISBN (audiobook): 979-8-9989633-3-9

Author Photo by William Kidston Photography
All story photos are the Author's personal photos taken during her journey.

Cover Graphic: Design Team Lynne, Ayman, and Xavier
Cover Design by the Author
Itinerary Illustration by Rick Gibson
Layout Design: Dawn Black

First Edition: June 2025
10 9 8 7 6 5 4 3 2

# DEDICATION

In loving memory of Ken Cortland, for teaching me to
follow my heart.

*No matter how hard I fall, I always land on my feet.*
*Sometimes kind of hard, but always on my feet.*

**-Reyna Clare**

# PRAISE

## THE YEAR I FELL INTO FRANCE

"Mel is very persuasive, showing how it is up to each of us to take the plunge and explore the world that is waiting 'out there', and how to set about it. And WWOOFing is one of the best ways of living in a country or region 'For Real' rather than floating over the surface as a tourist—not to mention all the fascinating and useful things you can learn."

Susan Coppard, Founder
Worldwide Opportunities on Organic Farms (WWOOF)

"When we are little, we are full of wonderment and discovery; everyday looking for something new to unfold. Mel's new book is a wonderful journey that stirs up our curiosity for magical living. This book will take you on a well needed adventure."

Tim Storey
Author, Speaker and the Original Comeback Coach

# The Year I Fell Into France

*France*

## My Recession-Proof
## Volunteer Journey

Mel Reyna Scott

# CONTENTS

# OPENING THOUGHTS

A tip to remember as you read my story. My volunteer trip was right before the smartphone and tablet explosion, before technology had advanced as we know it today. I was not (at the time) a gadget junky and didn't own a tablet, so my Blackberry was the only piece of technology I brought. I also put my mobile account on hold, my carrier's international calling and data plan was beaucoup expensive. This meant Wi-Fi only, with no texting, and phone calls to family were at a minimum. Most importantly, this also meant I had no translation app to assist me, and I did my translation the old-fashioned way *with a paperback French dictionary*.

The blog quotes throughout this book are from *Life Patrol*, my blog that my family and friends forced me to start when I announced my trip. I quickly learned that the cell service at many of the WWOOFing locations was almost nonexistent, and I would have limited or no access to a computer. And even when I did, the Internet service was so sporadic I could only post blog posts at Internet cafés while moving from one location to another. I would hand-write my post, usually while sitting at a local café drinking a glass of house wine and eating a croissant. (Had I known the future of influencing, I could have become one of the original travel influencers.)

# ITINERARY

## GOOD GRIEF
# With a Smile on My Face

Panic suddenly struck when my plane landed at Charles De Gaulle, and the flight attendant began the welcome message of, "Wah-wah, wah wah wah, wah-wah." Her lips were moving but all I heard was Charlie Brown's teacher. I had been so excited for my first trip to France that I was awake for most of the redeye flight from JFK. I was too busy envisioning warm, buttery croissants and handsome French princes sweeping me off my feet to notice that all the in-flight announcements up to that point had been in English.

My palms began to sweat as we taxied to the gate and I felt like I was being 'Punked.' After all, I knew French. Well… sort of. I had not only taken French in high school but also went through a three-month Adult Ed course before I boarded the plane. I even put French lessons on my phone that I had religiously listened to daily. I knew how to say, "I would like," so I had been confident I would be able to at least get myself a glass of wine and a ham and cheese sandwich. But now, I wasn't so sure, as I felt completely alienated in a foreign land I'd only been in for two whopping minutes. *Holy shit,* a part of me screamed from within. *What was I thinking?*

As I deplaned, I followed the crowd in front of me and quickly spotted the suitcase sign, feeling a small wave of relief. I would at least be able to find my way to baggage claim. As I walked through the terminal, looking at all the signs in the stores and food stands, I was still hearing "Wah-wah" in the background. I even went into a bookstore to test my wits and grabbed the nearest magazine, only to find myself completely blank. As if I was an archeologist dusting off a tablet from Egyptian civilization, trying to determine what exactly I had just found. Yes, it was official: I had no French language skills whatsoever.

I stopped to look around at all the people in the terminal, going about their business as if it were just another travel day. Parents shushing crying babies, businesspeople feverishly checking emails, elderly grandparents patiently waiting to be greeted by their grandkids. Everyone looked so calm and normal. Was I the only one petrified, alone, and unable to understand a word anyone was saying?

Six months prior, I was finally finding a sense of closure over my failed marriage as I celebrated my two-year divorce-aversary and was beginning to get my life back on track. After struggling to save every penny and upon concluding exhaustive research on solutions for the debt my divorce conveniently left me, I declared bankruptcy and started my rebuild from scratch. I still wasn't clear on how I had gone from having a comfortable life in the burbs with a real estate portfolio worth nearly one million on paper to being a broke divorcee living in a five-bedroom *Friends* house with four roommates, paying alimony to someone making nearly three times what I was (don't ask) and a dinky office job in midtown. But there I was, slowly putting building blocks on top of one another, recalibrating and navigating my way through life once again. It meant imagining my life anew and day-dreaming as I once had when I was young. Up first was to somehow embark on a dream trip to France with my girlfriends for my fortieth birthday. And by the next year, relocate to L.A.

But… life once again had its own plan. One fine mid-December afternoon, while I was at my cubicle planning the next week's mani-pedi client meetings for the sales team, the news was broken to me that my position was being relocated from New York to DC. Before I could even begin to process this information, the conversation conveniently flowed into "You are welcome to apply, although your skills don't match the new job description." Blind-sidedness seemed to be the new life norm… I don't recall the remainder of that conversation; I was too transfixed by my immediate physical reaction—I was smiling. My lips had stretched into a giant smile, and all I could hear was my inner monologue, *Why am I smiling right now? I'm being laid off! What's wrong with me?*

As the meeting ended, reality began sinking in. "Oops," life said to me while I stared back at it with a smiling "joke's on you" poker face. Within a single meeting, the new thread of hope I had recently found for myself snapped like a dry-rotted rubber band.

I left the office that afternoon stunned. I needed a drink. I immediately called my friend Jon to ask him to join me for our favorite dive bar happy hour. I had a lot to unpack, and he was the perfect person to unpack with. Jon had his fair share of experiences in life and would understand me better than anyone else, mainly because he had lost his job recently as well. And not once, but twice in the same year.

I was almost sprinting down the NYC sidewalks, and if I could have run off the earth, I would have. Which, now when I think back, could be the reason why I didn't notice the bitter sundown winter winds whipping around the tall buildings. Or perhaps pure numbness had set in by then. There were pangs of anger that were swelling up inside me, a pure sense of bewilderment and sheer terror. I was in the land of OZ, frantically looking for my red shoes.

"Life has a weird way of surprising us, Mel. Everything happens for a reason. At the end of the day, it all works out," Jon said with a warm smile as he sat down next to me. As nice as that sounded, it felt far off from my reality. It took me a few drinks to wash away the emotional charge and initial layer of shock I was still in, and that is when I revealed to him how I wanted to celebrate my upcoming birthday in France. And of all the things I could be upset about in this situation, it was my first trip to France that was breaking my heart the most. I shared with him my fascination for anything French from a young age. My love for cheese, art, and music, and the fresh scents of bakeries that I envisioned. It was like presenting my case in the court of life and appealing for justice. The romantic within me felt the idea dissolving into thin air. I would have to let go of my dream trip even before it had a chance to be booked. I felt even more helpless at that moment than I had the day I moved out of my newly renovated house still occupied by my ex.

But Jon said something that lit a small spark of hope deep inside me. "If you truly want to experience the spirit of France, why don't you go and live there?" His words flowed like a river of wisdom with strong yet calm certainty. "That's the only way you will truly get to know the country and the people." He would know—he had lived in Japan for five years. And he had a great point. The adventure and learning experience of new places is about the culture, whether it's a new city or a foreign country. I always seek out everyday life adventures when I go somewhere new. I love to feel what it's like to live somewhere else and hang out with the locals, not the touristy, pretty, picture-perfect stuff. Living in France would be idyllic and a great way to finally learn the beautiful language.

I sat quietly and consciously, allowing that to sink in... *live in France...* My heart was registering it, but my mind was taking its time to accept. *Live in France?* As amazing as that sounded, it felt like an impossible idea. How the hell was I going to pull that off? It reminded me of when my ex-husband had said I thought of life as a movie and he had made me question my dreams and whether I was living in a world that was unrealistic. And now here I was... dreaming up France as my new movie. Maybe I was living in an unrealistic dream world. But, then again, I had nothing to lose at that point. Why shouldn't I do what I want? I felt as if my brain was being pulled and stretched in a taffy puller, and I could only focus on one thought at a time. And that thought was that I wanted to live in France. As crazy and impossible as it felt, I decided that night—right there in the bar—that this was what I wanted to do. Building a space rocket seemed easier to figure out than how I would pull it off, but my decision had been made.

I was still in a state of shock as I left, but a glimmer of childlike happiness washed over me as gratitude began to build inside. I was grateful to have wonderful friends, grateful to have a newfound freedom most people never experience, and grateful to have found a positive perspective on a heartbreaking situation. Jon had surrounded me with exciting, dreamlike perspectives—ones I never would have come up with on my own. He had given me hope, and now I was about to say, "Au revoir, old life and bonjour new adventures!"

The question was—*how*?

# A WWOOF IS BORN
## Adventurers Only Need Apply

Hungover and still numb inside, I sat at my desk, staring at my inbox, trying not to vomit into my trashcan. Unsure if the nausea was the hangover or the empty pit left inside from yesterday's torpedo.

My numbness gradually turned into full-blown terror with every passing and excruciating hour. All I could think about was that I didn't know where I was going to go from here or how I would get there. I felt claustrophobic by my own life. My move-to-France idea, as irrational and crazy as it sounded, began to feel like the best way out of the black hole I had just fallen into. Strangely enough, it quickly started to grow into the only ounce of sanity that brought a twinge of comfort to me that day, and I clung to it for dear life.

I spent the next two weeks researching possible options, desperately trying to figure out how to make this trip happen. I still considered it a berserk idea, even preposterous at times, and honestly thought it would take a miracle to come to fruition. But I also knew in my heart it was exactly what I wanted. So I kept at it every day—brainstorming ideas and surfing the web. Based on my "working in France" research, I quickly determined that working there (legally, anyway) was going to be virtually impossible. The visas, paperwork, blah, blah, blah.

Randomly one day my click landed on www.WWOOF. net. It's now called Worldwide Opportunities on Organic Farms, but at that time, it was called "Willing Workers on Organic Farms."

As I scanned the website, my heart started pounding, and excitement butterflies began fluttering in my stomach. There are both WWOOFing hosts and WWOOFing volunteers. WWOOFing hosts provide room and board in exchange for the volunteers to work an average of four to five hours per day at their farm, business, etc. The only expense a WWOOFer incurs is getting oneself to and from the host location. There are WWOOFing organizations worldwide, and for around $25 per year, you can become a member of the country of your choice and have access to the entire hosting database. There is no limit to the number of countries you join; it's completely up to you and your budget. Volunteering really is that simple.

*Wow, I might have found a way to live in France for practically nothing. Four or five hours of volunteer work a day, with meals and lodging included... seriously?* I quickly told myself the site had to be an Internet scheme. It just seemed too good to be true. But the more I read, the more I realized it was a legitimate organization established in England in 1971 by a woman named Susan Coppard, and it was very real.

Imagine working on a vineyard in the south of France while learning to speak French and seeing the beautiful countryside. It was like the movie *French Kiss*; I could go live the movie! Well at least the vineyard part; and pray for the hot guy to appear. I signed up immediately and officially became a French WWOOFer.

I printed the entire host database the next day at work, created a three-inch thick binder, and began my homework that night. There were over 150 hosts, and each had a paragraph or two describing their location and usually listed the WWOOFing responsibilities they needed help with.

For the next three weeks, including most of my Christmas break, I researched. About half of the database was in French, and only about a quarter had websites. I quickly ran out of patience trying to read and translate the French-only listings. The online translators were not getting the complete gist of what was written. I decided to focus on the host descriptions that were in English, especially those with a website. Some of them were pretty straightforward and painted a clear picture. Others you had to read between the lines and really think about what they were saying. I felt some were mainly looking for volunteers to take care of chickens and/or children the whole time. Those I immediately knew weren't for me. Not to mention the basket weaving and the animal cleanup crew locations. No, thank you.

In addition to scrutinizing the descriptions, my research also included looking up each location on the map to see where exactly it was. Other than Paris and Cannes, I knew little about France's geography and was curious about each location I read about. This realization prompted me to get professional help. Who better to teach me about France than the traveling guru Rick Steves? I went straight to Idlewild Books, a travel-themed bookshop in Manhattan, and bought his France guidebook.

By New Year's Eve, my WWOOFing binder was packed full of highlighted, tabbed, and ranked entries. My binder,

Rick Steves's book, and overall excitement became my holy trinity. Since I'm a hopeless romantic, any vineyard automatically got moved to the top of the selection ladder. I also found two locations that were hosting theater events, which appealed to me because, a few years earlier, I decided to take a stab at acting. It had always been a hidden dream. That was why I had taken the job in NYC, so I would be conveniently in the city all day and could easily and quickly get to all my auditions. I had booked a few tiny parts in infomercials and student films but I had not, thus far, "been discovered." Being a movie star wannabe, I wasn't going to live in France without meeting some actors and experiencing French summer theater.

The WWOOFing program itself does not schedule any of the volunteer assignments for you or provide transportation to and from locations. It simply gives you access to the database and hosts' information. It's your responsibility to correspond with the hosts directly and get them to "accept" you. I toiled for several days crafting my sales pitch for a non-French-speaking manual labor spot.

Now, being a coal miner's daughter from West Virginia, I've spent some afternoons in the garden and have "roughed it" a time or two. My parents had grown a vegetable garden every summer that had more square footage than our house. I also own my own toolbox and am quite handy around the house. I included pictures of home improvements and landscaping I had done on my ex-house to showcase my strengths. I eventually narrowed it down to my top twenty host choices and e-mailed my applications.

Keep in mind that applying is like job hunting. Only half of the hosts will respond, and there is plenty of rejection. Some were already booked for the dates I requested, and others flat-out told me they didn't think I was a good match. Those who responded positively provided me with directions on how to locate them, what they would expect of me work-wise, and overall information about their business or residence. The correspondence varied from simple pleasantries and date confirmations to downright hilarious entertainment. I could tell Adele in Burgundy had a great sense of humor as she referred to her home as a "crumbling heap." I couldn't wait to meet her. The vegetable farmer, Paul, stated his farm was somewhat primitive and without hot water or a shower; he wasn't sure it was the place for me. I simply told him that I came from the country and could handle roughing it. I had been without hot water before. I was only staying a week. How bad could it be?

That conversation did, however, prompt me to be sure to include a few nights on my own in hotels in between some of the WWOOFing locations. I figured I might need a little R&R at some point, and there were a few "not to miss" items on my list. Like the Champagne region, the Riviera, Giverny, and the first-ever Impressionism Festival in Normandy. I'd loved Monet since Ms. Poling's art appreciation class in high school. Not only would I be going to the Lily Pond, but Monet's work would be plastered in museums all over Normandy for the entire summer. It would be an Impressionistic heaven.

By late February, after two and a half months of WWOOFing research, mileage calculations, and calendar roulette, my itinerary had fallen into place as the last of the responses rolled in. I had six confirmed hosts, all of which would only commit to two weeks or less, and some had certain dates that they needed filled and weren't so flexible. So, I molded the dates and locations into one giant travel loop around the country. That way, I would not be backtracking, and there wouldn't be long travel times between locations. The train pricing was also less expensive for shorter trips, so it made sense all around doing it that way.

My first WWOOFing destination was a château in the Picardy region. There was going to be an art festival while I was there, and the château looked absolutely beautiful. The other WWOOFing locations included two vineyards (one where the owners didn't speak English—that was going to be interesting), Simone in Parthenay, who didn't have a business but simply needed help with her garden, Paul and Marie at the vegetable farm in Saint-Girons, Marq and Paige in Torsac who needed help with a theater festival, and Adele at the B&B in Burgundy.

In addition to the WWOOFing locations and the Impressionism Festival, I planned to visit Paris and the Riviera. I would be gone from May through the end of August and was going to cover over 2,200 miles while staying in fourteen different towns/regions: Paris, Picardy, Reims, Amboise, Parthenay, Torsac, Saint-Émilion, Bizanet, Saint-Girons, Toulon, Antibes, Vauvert, Marcheseuil, and Rouen. It was official: I was leaving for France in less than three months.

*Now what?*

## LIFE PATROL
# The Push and Pull

As with many new ideas, especially those out of the box, one finds that friends are generally supportive. Luckily, I have the world's best friends and was surrounded by unconditional validation, encouragement, and cheerleaders. My family, on the other hand, was a little slower to get on board. Mostly out of fear, I believe. I thought we would need to put my niece on an IV of Valium after she watched Taken.

I will admit, my family was not the only doubtful one. In truth, I had tried that entire spring to avoid all the fear, pain, and worthlessness I felt. I am often good at hiding my emotions and putting on a game face; I have done this my whole life. But, after I found out I was losing this job, I had to forcibly use the "I'm just fine" mask so that everyone would assume I was OK. But at the end of the day, I was alone and scared. I couldn't even begin to think about how I would support myself for the rest of my life or how I would build a new retirement nest egg. At that point, all I had were my clothes, a few pieces of furniture, and what was left of my sanity. When I got divorced, I left my house, my cat, everything—I had just wanted out.

As I analyzed my life, I had never felt like I fit in, nor had a clear vision of what I wanted to do when I "grew up." I had never felt "successful" or that I had accomplished much. The only two times I had felt normal and like a productive contributor to society were when I received my college degree and during my brief real estate investment success when I launched my real estate "empire" with a $14,000 down payment on a new construction Florida condo, sight unseen. This was while the bubble wand was still in the soap bottle. I was working as a real estate agent selling new construction in New Jersey. A friend of mine was looking to move there and had been to the Florida site. She thought it looked confidently promising. I spent a month researching online and had multiple phone calls with local realtors before signing the contract... I saw my retirement condo unit one hour prior to closing.

By the time the bubble had hit its max, I had turned my $14,000 investment into a $100,000 paper profit, and my combined real estate investments were worth over $800,000. I had my retirement home and a residual income in place. Then the bubble burst, thus my divorce and bankruptcy.

The more I thought about these things and the more I analyzed myself, I felt as if I might actually be going crazy. What was I thinking, taking off to live in France for four months? Who does that? And how in the hell was I going to pull it off? A) I was going by myself; B) I didn't speak the language; and C) I had never WWOOFed before. An emotional and mental train wreck didn't come close to describing me.

That said, I am an extremely independent person and not afraid of adventure. I am used to going places alone, for goodness sake, including foreign countries. I once took a trip by myself to Costa Rica to investigate a real estate opportunity. I love to explore and make new friends. Clearly, I have done this before, albeit on slightly more pleasant terms, but nonetheless, I wasn't the country bumpkin I had been twenty years earlier when I moved to New Jersey at twenty years old with no family nearby. So why exactly was I freaking out? This trip was, after all, the only positive thing in my life at that time and certainly the only thing that brought any level of happiness to my soul. But I had questions that kept looping themselves through my head about this trip: *What kind of experiences would I have there? What type of people would I meet? Would I be able to get myself from place to place, speaking minimal French? What was I going to do when I got back home? Where would I live?* On and on and on.

Finally one day I decided to schedule an appointment with someone I was confident would give me a straight-up, unbiased answer whether I should really do this or not. I had taken a course at the Sam Christensen Studio of Los Angeles with Ken and Sam right at the time my marriage ended, and I completely trusted their opinions and advice. Luckily for me, they happened to be in town that week, and Ken had an opening in his schedule. I saw him the next day.

I briefly outlined my story to him and explained my plan to live in France. I told him how several people basically told me I was crazy and how, in a matter of a few years, my whole life had fallen apart. He smiled, and calmly and very matter of factly, told me, "You are not crazy. All the people who are looking at you like you are crazy are the people who aren't following their hearts and aren't going after their dreams. What you're doing appears crazy to them because they can't imagine doing it themselves. As for your life falling apart, sometimes your life has to fall apart before it can fall together. You are simply following your heart, and there is nothing whatsoever crazy about that. Go to France and have a great time."

That was, and is to this day, one of the most powerful conversations I've had in my life. It allowed me to understand that you can follow advice, you can follow your best plan, you can follow the rules, and you can even follow others. But in the end, you can't really follow anything but your heart.

By the time my departure rolled around, my family had accepted my decision and given me their blessings. After all, they had no choice; I was going hell or high water. I did, however, take safety precautions. My cousin Sue and I created what we called the "FBI File." I sent her my itinerary with phone numbers, addresses and e-mails of my hosts, as well as the hotel reservations. So if I disappeared, she would know where to start looking. I also bought a key chain mace. (Only to forget it under my pillow in hotel number two.)

This trip also meant I needed to give up my *Friends* room. I knew in my heart that when I returned from France, I wanted to live in California. That was where I wanted to hang my new shingle on life. Why not? I had no more ties holding me to New York. As for acting, my biggest claim to fame was some background work on a soap opera. And there certainly wasn't any love connection begging me to stay.

So for the second time in two years, I packed my life into a storage unit and officially became a vagabond, living out of a suitcase with no commitments in tow. I had complete freedom.

## JE PARLE ANGLAIS
### Don't Worry, I Planned for That

"Welcome to France, madame," said the customs agent, frank yet with a welcoming smile, as she put the France stamp into my passport.

Luckily a small miracle had happened as I made my way to baggage claim—my suitcase came down the conveyor belt as soon as I stepped up to grab my spot along the edge. No lost luggage! I had taken a beat in an attempt to calm my nerves and allow the realization to sink in that I was going to be here for the next four months as a WWOOFer volunteer. When I originally planned this trip, four months seemed like such a short time, and now, it felt like an eternity. As I got myself settled down, I fell into a slight state of relaxation where my heart was no longer beating out of my chest and I was breathing somewhat normally. My choices were clear; I could turn around and go back home or I could stay and have what might be the most remarkable adventure of my life. So I had carried on to customs.

I will admit on one hand, as the ink was drying, it felt quite adventurous that I would go on about my day without knowing any proper French. Isn't this what the adventure of a new place is all about? You visit the unknown without knowing your way and figure it out as you go. At the end of the day, you survive, experience something new, and live to tell the tale. Ultimately, I've always managed to land on my feet. Yet this time, it felt like the carpet had been yanked from underneath me, and I was clueless about where I was going to land on this one.

So I told myself, *Fuck it. You're a 40-year-old grown woman. You got this.* After all, there was nothing and no one to go home to. Giving in to my fight-or-flight response, I decided to suck it up, put on my big-girl panties, grabbed my 59.5-pound suitcase, and set out to find the metro that would take me to my hotel, permitting life to run its course. Besides, at this point, I was too jet-lagged to bog down into details. For now, I had to focus on the fact that I had landed in a foreign country where I didn't speak the language, had no idea what my WWOOFing adventure was going to be like, or how I was going to successfully communicate with anyone. All I knew was that I would figure it out—starting with finding an ATM for some Euros and determining how to get my ridiculously heavy suitcase that I could barely maneuver onto the metro.

I curiously enough managed to get through it without asking for help. The metro was easier to figure out than the first time I rode the NYC subway, and it was certainly much cleaner. It looked new with fresh paint and didn't have any of those mystery odors I was accustomed to.

The car took off quickly and felt like an effortless motion. There was none of the jerking and swerving that my now "ex-morning NYC commute" used to have. The smoothness and quiet of the ride began to calm me. I slowly released the clenching of my jaw as I looked out the train window, anxiously searching for a glimpse of the Eiffel Tower. I began to feel a twinge of excitement and hope. Maybe I would be OK, and this journey I had put myself on could be an adventure with exciting unknowns and endless possibilities. Perhaps I would fall in love, find a great job, and never come home—or at least eat delicious food and pastries. Anything was possible, if I believed it to be.

I had a solid fifteen minutes of calm, hopefulness, and self-preservation as the train rolled closer to the City of Love. Unfortunately, it didn't take long for the panic to return. The metro stop for my hotel was closed. The train stopped one station short, and everyone had to disembark. I dragged my too-heavy suitcase to the top of the metro stairs and onto the sidewalk. I was standing in the middle of a foreign country with no one to call for help. My heart was racing out of my chest, and I was right back to square one.

My first views of Paris were supposed to be fun, exciting, and full of adventurous life, not terror, fright, and complete emotional chaos. I had no idea where I was or which direction I needed to go. I had mapped out my route to the hotel using the metro; those were the only instructions I had written down, and I had no phone. I had planned so carefully, and now here I was, standing alone on a Paris sidewalk, feeling completely exposed and helpless. Not to mention angry, I would have to spend my first Euros on a taxi instead of a quaint afternoon at a sidewalk café like a tourist should be doing. This planning thing didn't seem to be something that worked out for me and my life.

Thankfully, it was a beautiful sunny day and hailing a cab was easy. I had the printout of the hotel, so I didn't have to do much for the driver to understand where to go. As he took off he began to speak in broken English, which was a relief. At least I understood a few words. But that relief didn't last long either, as it was the scariest cab ride of my life. The speeding, the swerving, being jerked back and forth, the cab driver honking, yelling, and running red lights. It was nuts. I was so scared I don't even remember if I wore my seatbelt or not. Hell, I don't even remember if the cab even had a seatbelt. I had experienced NYC for twenty years and never had such a horrible cab driver. I finally understood how my family had felt when they rode in a cab for the first time while visiting me and they were totally freaked out. I felt bad that I had downplayed their fear because I surely knew what they were talking about now.

To my amazement, I made it to my hotel in one piece. And, bonus, the front-desk lady spoke fluent English. I was so happy I wanted to hug her! I checked my suitcase and took off as fast as I could. I was mentally and physically exhausted but wasn't about to waste my day sleeping. I had made it that far and by damn, I was in Paris, and I was going to enjoy it. Besides, my adrenaline was so high at that point I couldn't have slept anyway.

It was nightmarishly clear I wasn't going to be able to read simple signs in store windows and train stations or brochures at hotels. All these are key aspects that I didn't truly consider would be an issue until I began to maneuver myself around that day. You don't realize how much you take for granted in your everyday life or while traveling in your own country until you leave and discover it's not so easy. When I had gone to Costa Rica, all I had to do was get myself to the hotel and meet up with a group. I didn't have to worry about directions. While everyone in the group was strangers, I wasn't alone. So technically, this was my first time going to a foreign-language country with no one greeting me or touring me around. Which meant that every day was a French lesson in one way or another, between the products, magazines, TV, newspapers, and of course, menus.

I suppose my forced optimistic attitude worked because that very first day in Paris, as I walked the sidewalks for hours gawking at the architecture, I was stopped four times by people asking in French for what I believe were directions. Four times! I simply said, "Je parle Anglais," and everyone understood that I was a tourist. I wasn't sure what exactly made me look like a local, but I took it as a compliment. It brought a few moments of comfort and joy to my day, which was severely needed and welcomed after the way it had started.

The next day was my first full day in Paris before leaving for my first WWOOFing location, and to my dismay, I awoke to cold rain. And by cold rain, I mean the bone-chilling kind you expect in Seattle. I had not packed for this - wasn't it summertime? I layered up in hopes of keeping warm and, thankfully, did have an umbrella, so off I went to explore. As I attempted to sightsee while shivering, I got the idea of bakery hopping to help keep myself warm. It works for bars, so why not patisseries? I have a sweet tooth the size of Texas, so I decided I would create a pastry treasure-hunt adventure everywhere I went for my entire trip.

I can't talk about pastries, of course, without mentioning the chocolate croissant. It was one of the first things I ate upon arrival and continued to eat throughout my stay. It's one of those staples that never disappoints. Always consistent, always available, and "to-go" friendly. I had more in those four months than I have had my entire life. It will forever be my go-to choice.

I have been a chocoholic since birth, so I decided to broaden my horizons and made sure to occasionally try things outside the chocolate box. I constantly scouted out new macaron flavors and left no bakery unturned, looking for unique pastries that I'd never eaten before.

I began this quest out of the gate when I found "dots" for breakfast that morning. They were like a flat éclair with less filling, but just as delicious. Even with the freezing rain, day two was starting off perfectly.

I made my way to the Galeries Lafayette but quickly lost patience. It is a popular department store and apparently a hot spot. Like many touristy places, it was crowded and full of tourists. I lasted only an hour and quickly decided I was more interested in the sights of Paris than wasting time inside stores. I would have much more fun scouting out the cafés and architecture that the city had to offer. My shopping thrills are bargains and hidden treasures, so

I saved shopping for the French markets everyone always raves about and knew I would eventually find along the way.

That afternoon would launch my forever go-to, most enjoyable lunch in France—cheese. Le fromage is my second love only to chocolate and champagne and bread. When I travelled on my own between WWOOFing stops and walking around a town playing tourist, I would often make my own lunch of a pâté and cheese sandwich. Both bakeries and cheese shops were never hard to find, and all the cheese shops I went to also sold pâté. I would usually pick a spot nearby that had benches or some kind of ledge to sit on and people-watch while I ate.

14/05/2010

My first lunch in Paris was sitting in a park gazing at the Eiffel Tower, eating what tasted like the best lunch of my life. Funny story—I have no idea what park I was in and have yet to find where I was that day! I had hopped onto the metro and randomly selected a stop. Maybe Rick Steves could help with that one.

Blog post: *Recommended dosage*

*The French twist to morning barhopping: bakery hopping. Begin with one chocolate éclair. Gradually add a seasonal fruit tart. Top with six various macaron flavors. Quantity may increase depending upon dinner and wine intake to follow. As with any new regimen, please consult your local pastry chef for correct dosage. Results (AKA pants size) will vary. \*\*There were no waistbands harmed while researching this post.*

The macaron flavors were far from my normal flavor palate, which made it so much fun trying them all. My top favorites were violet, lavender, pistachio, chestnut, and rose, with lavender winning the top slot. It had a hint of bitterness hidden within its sugar explosion.

The "most unique macaron venue" was the McDonald's in Paris I found that afternoon. You know you're in the motherland of pastries when Micky D's has a counter of them. There were two sides to the restaurant: the regular hamburger side and the coffee/dessert side. It had a modern symmetrical design and felt like McDonalds met Starbucks met the Starship Enterprise.

# CRYING WWOOF
## Up and At 'Em

Anyone in fear of being bored while WWOOFing, fear not. From digging up a sleeping groundhog in the garden to fighting chickens in the backyard, there was always something crazy fun going on to keep it interesting. It took me a week in Picardy to figure out that it wasn't a cuckoo clock inside the house I was hearing every day; it was real cuckoo birds in the trees outside. They drove me bananas.

I am happy with all the WWOOFing locations I chose. I never went hungry (some of the most delicious food I've ever tasted), and I always had a roof over my head—not always a warm one, but a roof nonetheless. All locations were safe and, in their own way, supplied you with everything you needed to exist. I had a comfy bed and hot shower at all but one of my locations and that one I knew about beforehand. Every host took great care of us WWOOFers and obliged our requests as best they could. I learned and saw so many things, and most importantly, I met some very fine people. I believe a destination is what you make it. It doesn't matter whether it's two towns over or halfway around the world. I believe one's experiences will only be as good as you allow them to be.

When I was organizing my schedule, I chose an eclectic mix of locations to get a well-rounded viewpoint of everyday living. That said, most of the work I did generally consisted of cleaning, pruning, and general gardening activities, with some jobs being more fun than others. Thanks to the perpetual frosty cold weather, wet outdoor chores were as common as croissants. With the exception of Southern France, it was cold and raining almost everywhere I went, thus I was cold and miserable eighty percent of the time. I heard over and over again throughout my travels that the weather was unseasonably cool. Leave it to me to completely change the climate of an entire country. Had there been a fleece man there, I would have married him; I hate being cold. One of the many jokes on me: thinking summers would be warm in France. It was as cold as San Francisco that year.

Rain also meant I was covered in mud—daily. I quickly learned to stop trying to keep my clothes clean, it was a wasted effort. Same for any type of hair styling and makeup. There was no need for any of that most days. Nothing could be done about Mother Nature; she runs her own show, so I worked in wet, cold, muddy clothes many days.

The WWOOFing job definitions varied as much as the work itself. To some, "clearing a field" meant mowing grass by hand. To others, it was minor lumberjacking without saws. And of course, one cannot forget about the weeding. I did more weeding in four months than my entire childhood gardening stint. Even at the vineyards, I pulled out large weeds between the vines, almost as big as the vines themselves. If WWOOF were to give weeding certifications, I would have received one.

Task communication methods varied among the other WWOOFing locations. Some hosts would write down instructions, while others would discuss them with you over breakfast that day or even at dinner the night before. Regardless, they always made sure you knew what they needed you to work on and get completed.

The daily WWOOFing time schedule was similar at most locations. The mornings started early, between 7:00 a.m. and 8:00 a.m. working through until lunch, followed by a couple of hours of downtime, or what most referred to as the afternoon "siesta." Then another three or four more hours of work in the late afternoon until dinner. Regardless of the location I was at, by the time a siesta came around, I welcomed it. Not necessarily because I was exhausted from the day's work, but the quiet time was a great opportunity to decompress and hang out with other WWOOFers. There were a few WWOOFers that kept to themselves, but most were lots of fun to be around and had great stories to tell. Depending upon your length of stay and location, you usually get a day off every five days or so. Some days, I went on adventures by myself; other times, a group of us would go as a WWOOFing posse to explore and have fun. As for the number of WWOOFers at each location, some hosts preferred to have only one at a time, while others needed several WWOOFers year-round.

The thing is, you aren't going to know exactly what you will experience while WWOOFing until you get there and you're in the thick of it. That goes for the work you will be doing as well as the overall adventures you will have. Just trust you will have fun, learn lots of new things, meet lovely new people, and see parts of the world you may have never seen before otherwise.

## CHARADES
## Whatever. Je Parle Française

Smiles and laughter are universal. I can confidently say that despite my first-day experiences, I truly had a blast breaking the language barrier and that the ups far outweighed the downs. One of the prominent communication lessons I learned is that people do not need to speak the same language to successfully communicate. Language itself is one piece of the communication jigsaw puzzle, and each word is a clue. Like with my taxi driver, sometimes simply showing the paper with my hotel and address did the trick. Eventually, you connect a few pieces of the border, and while you don't know what was said verbatim, you understand the concept and understand the big picture. It is actually a fun adventure within itself, as long as you choose to make it so.

I must emphasize here the inaccuracy of the rude French stereotype. Out of the entire restaurant, train station, and everyday language encounters throughout, I only had one rude stereotypical experience. It was in a Parisian café when I was making my attempt to speak French to the cashier. The lady snared at me and coldly said, "You can speak English." I have to tell you that I was so relieved to speak without having to think that I didn't care she had just been obnoxious to me. Unbeknownst to her, she had actually made my day a little easier.

I was fortunate enough to have many kind people help me learn throughout my journey. I would sometimes get corrected as I spoke, but usually in a positive and supportive manner. And I'm talking all the people that I met, from waiters to complete strangers to WWOOFing hosts. Most hosts were gracious about my language impediment, and all but one were patient and did their best to help all the non-French speaking WWOOFers to learn. That said, I learned that all hosts did prefer WWOOFers spoke French whenever possible. Some were stricter than others when it came to daily conversation, but luckily, none of them went completely by the "speak only French" rule. They couldn't if they wanted me to understand exactly what they were saying. This was not an expectation I had of them; it was simply reality if they really wanted me to understand what they needed me to do. In truth, I didn't understand anything I heard most of my trip.

As I moved on average every ten days from one WWOOF location to the next while mixing in sightseeing stops, I soon caught on that in touristy cities like Paris and Amboise, people spoke English at the hotels, restaurants, and train stations. I could cheat during those moments, but once I got out into the country and the smaller towns and villages, forget it—*no one* spoke English. That is where charades came in handy.

## PICARDY
## Just Open A Window

I had entered into this trip with the thought that, regardless of how good or bad a WWOOFing location was, I would only be there a week or two. If I didn't like it, the time would go by quickly. And my first location was, well, let's just say, "interesting."

My two-week shift was at a family-owned château in the heart of the Picardy region just north of Paris and only about an hour by train. The small town was quaint and picturesque. Picture the French version of Norman Rockwell. Now, even though I grew up surrounded by mountains and fields, I'm a city girl at heart and not normally impressed by country scenes. I'm more interested in architecture or the beach. So it takes a lot to excite me when it comes to the countryside. Well, hello! The yellow fields of canola that were near the château were the most beautiful fields I have ever seen in my life. It looked as if the Impressionists had spread yellow paint all across them. The color was bright, perfectly blended, and absolutely stunning. I loved gazing at them and took them in every chance I got.

I had only been in France for three days, and needless to say, I hadn't learned a word of French. Yet to my joy, getting to Picardy was a breeze. I took the metro to the train station and miraculously found my train without issue. Olivia, my host, had an arrangement with a private driver for all of her WWOOFers to use. He was reasonably priced, spoke English, and was at the Picardy train station waiting on me as promised. Olivia greeted me as I arrived and welcomed me to her home—in English. She appeared to be in her mid-fifties and seemed pleasant enough to me. However, soon after the other WWOOFers, all English speakers, quickly pulled me aside to tell me, "Try to speak French whenever possible." *Yeah*, I thought, *no problem. I know at least three whole sentences.* She had greeted me in English—I wasn't quite sure what the others were trying to tell me until the next day.

When I came down for breakfast, our daily chore list was written in French—not one word was in English. I quickly learned to bring my dictionary with me each morning. As time progressed, it was apparent that Olivia wasn't a patient person when it came to speaking French and was obviously agitated when we didn't understand what she was saying when she spoke to us. It wasn't that she refused to speak English, but she wasn't overly coddling about us not understanding.

The other WWOOFers and I managed to put a fun spin on this stressful experience though and made flash cards complete with colored pencil illustrations. We also played French-only Scrabble while fully utilizing our dictionaries. I felt like a child in a sink-or-swim environment being forced to study for a test. It was beyond nerve-racking but at the same time, it was also great for learning. I actually retained a tiny piece of new vocabulary, what else but "désherber" (the French verb meaning "to weed").

While châteaus are a dime a dozen in France, this one was my first and I was mesmerized. Compared to large royal palaces I read about, Olivia's château was the size of a pindrop. Yet, it had a story all its own and always found a way to impress me. It had been in Olivia's family for several generations. She told us WWOOFers the story about her childhood and how, at one time, her family had owned half of the village. After WWII, the properties had been auctioned off by the government. So her ancestors were able to buy land and châteaus inexpensively. Eventually, when her elders had passed, the château was left to her and her siblings. She was the only one interested in keeping the homestead, so she bought them out and kept it for herself.

One childhood story that impacted me greatly was how she had servants when she was growing up and that she never stepped foot inside the kitchen. If she wanted something, she asked for it, and it was brought to her. This, of course, was completely outside of my reality and nothing I could relate to. For Olivia, she had experienced both sides of the gamut—from servants to WWOOFers within her lifetime. It was also an affirmation of how life can change 180 degrees and that we often don't know the way things will turn out for us in the end. This caused an important realization for me: other people also experience a complete life turnaround and that losing the life as you know it, didn't just happen to me. I wasn't so different after all. It offered me a sliver of hope. If Olivia could make it work, I would be able to as well.

She hosted three to four WWOOFers at any given time during the summer months, but the workload would have easily justified more. The grounds were full of flower gardens, vegetable gardens, berry patches, fields of grass, trees, and a large lawn surrounding the château that required mowing each week. Everywhere you looked, there were chores to be done and way too much for Olivia to tackle alone. I can only imagine how many servants it took to maintain the property during her childhood.

Along with family history, the château had lots of fascinating structural history, and I was on a constant treasure hunt. I love antiques and old houses, imagining what it must have been like to live in them when they were brand new and what the people may have looked and dressed like in that period. So I made sure I absorbed as much as possible during my stay and constantly observed the tiny little things around me.

There were two full floors and a finished attic with nooks and crannies all over the place. Each room I went into had at least one original something in it with its own piece of history to tell, right down to the doorknobs and original keys.

My favorite treasures were the original windows, candle lanterns, the old dishes, and miscellany I found in the kitchen. There were old bouillon cube boxes, crocks, and gadgets I didn't recognize. The windows were the most intriguing. They taught me that window engineering is not one of my talents. I couldn't figure out how to open them for days. I finally had to have Olivia explain them to me. Twist, turn, pull, push; they were complicated…

The outside was full of fascinating things too. Olivia gave us a guided tour (in English) one afternoon. There was a buggy garage, multiple cellars, a pigeon coop, and one section of the yard had been a tennis court in the 1940s. You could tell that back in the day, when the château was in full swing, it was a stunner.

The iron gate keys were my favorite outdoor item. Each gate still had its original lock with its four-inch keys. I had never seen such giant keys! It was as if they were unlocking the past yet allowing us to live in the present. And like the windows, the gate keys and I didn't play nice. You had to insert the key exactly right or it wouldn't open. I was locked out a couple of times until someone opened the gate from the inside.

During my stay, I met and worked with several other WWOOFers. Some were there for one or two weeks, like Jiro, and others were there for several months, like Sarina. Jiro was from Japan. He was probably twenty years old and spoke very good English. He told us the story of how both his grandparents had survived the atomic bomb. They had lived in separate parts of the city and hadn't met until after the war. Jiro didn't offer elaborate details, but we could tell it was an important and proud aspect of his lineage, and he enjoyed telling us about it.

For me, I didn't need details to be in awe. Being only two degrees away from Jima survivors and their love story was absolutely captivating. Not an everyday occurrence I would expect to happen and one of many unforgettable moments of my journey. Unfortunately, Jiro left right after I arrived, and I didn't have an opportunity to hear more about Japan and everyday life there. On his last day I asked him to help me write a postcard to Jon. I thought he'd be surprised to receive a French postcard from me written in Japanese. (After I returned home, I learned I had written the letters so perfectly that he hadn't believed I actually wrote them myself. I may not be able to speak French, but apparently I can write some mean Japanese.)

Sarina from New Zealand had already been there for six weeks and was scheduled to leave right after me. She was one of the most well-rounded and mature twenty-two-year-olds whom I've ever met. One of those people that you enjoy having around and never get tired of. Sarina was also a true WWOOFer. I believe her passion and heart belonged to the arts, but for that moment, it was dairy farming. Her next location was a French-speaking dairy farm. So she was cramming like crazy to learn the language and prepare for her next leg. I was going to be in the same situation at one of the vineyards, and I prayed that it would start soaking in for me soon too.

Sarina got a head start on the farming by biking almost every morning at 6:00 a.m. to get our milk from the local dairy farmer. She relished getting up early and being the milk fetcher and would sometimes get to milk the cow herself. We utterly enjoyed having it for our breakfast.

Sarina was also one of the few people in my entire journey that I witnessed smoking and her cigarette breaks were pure entertainment. The care and precision she eluded as she rolled each one, complete with licking them all the way down the side to seal them up and gently pressing the ends to finish. It was my dad all over again with his tin can of Prince Albert. And she always made sure no one near her got hit in the face with smoke, which I so much appreciated. I rarely saw smokers *anywhere* else. And I am certainly not complaining about this, I detest smoke, so this was a pleasant surprise as I was anticipating a smoking frenzy across the entire country, especially in the cafés in Paris. An unconscious stereotype I didn't realize I had until I noticed it.

## ACCIDENTS HAPPEN
## Bruised and Battered

As with unknowns, accidents can arise. One week in, I had a minor bicycle accident that affected me the entire journey. Another WWOOFer, Jessica, and I had gone bike riding to a local Picardy village one afternoon. As we were leisurely riding on a quiet residential street, a teenager came flying out of his driveway on his bicycle and T-boned me. He came out of nowhere; I didn't even see him. I fell hard on my right side and was quite shaken up. It was not emergency-room I'm bleeding worthy, but it certainly was enough to throw my lower back out and knock the chain off the bike. Jessica

attempted to fix the chain, but I ended up pushing the bike home, barely able to walk and in great pain.

The bike was a simple one-speed, so between all the other WWOOFers, they were able to fix it. Unfortunately, my aching body was not so lucky. My right thigh was black for over two weeks, and there were days immediately following that I had extreme lower back pain. (Hindsight, it actually should have been an urgent care moment.) Weeding was excruciating, so Olivia was kind enough to let me do some cleaning inside the house, which allowed me to stay productive and avoid wanting to swallow a bottle of prescription pain meds (which I didn't have). It was here that I coined my slogan: "Red wine and Advil cures anything." It was how I survived the remainder of the trip.

I was in some level of pain at all times. While some days were better than others, many were downright painful. Which means all the adventures you are about to read contain some level of back pain; I just didn't constantly write about it. Otherwise, I would have to call the book 'Whining in France.'

I considered going home that night while lying in bed, but that consideration only lasted for about a day. I decided that I was too excited to see everything and that as long as I had a pulse, I was staying. I was living one of my life's dreams, and I wasn't about to leave. France had plenty of Advil and I would deal with it.

The injury did cause me to have to visit a few doctors because of this throughout my four months. The first visit was only a few days after it happened. Olivia didn't have a car and a taxi would have cost a small fortune, there were none nearby anyway, so I biked to the nearest orthopedist-type doctor in the tiny country town a few miles away. Olivia had gone to him before and said he could cure almost any pain. I'm not sure what type of doctor he was exactly, but he was the closest thing there was to a chiropractor, and the visit did help enough to get me moving again. No insurance needed, so no hassle and no paperwork, and his fee was very reasonable.

I later went on to visit chiropractors in both Antibes and Paris. Both doctors spoke fluent English and were wonderful, helping me tremendously and getting me out of immediate pain. They were also affordable and charged the same amount my chiropractors do at home. Dr. Guillaume Mary in Antibes had a great setup. His office was like any typical chiropractic office I have been to, with one exception: it was on the French Riviera — laid back and uber casual. Dr. Caroline Lambert's office was near the Arc de Triomphe and a bit more upscale and "Parisian." She had lived in Texas for a while and was lovely. I highly recommend them both if you're ever in France and need a good adjustment. I enjoy saying I have DC "people" in France; it gives me a good giggle.

## MEL THE MULE
## Weeding My Way

The WWOOFing jobs at Picardy were primarily focused on preparing the property for an art festival that Olivia was hosting, which was scheduled during my stay. Most days, we usually split the job assignments amongst ourselves and would venture off to go do our individual tasks. Other days, like field clearing assignments which were big jobs, we would complete as a group.

The work consisted mostly of weeding and clearing overgrown areas. Almost everything was done by hand, and what tools we did have were old and dull. And by clearing overgrown areas, I mean lumberjacking by hand and hand mowing the hay-like field with a scythe. You think I'm exaggerating the lumberjacking? There were several tree branches that had been cut down by a hired gardener and left on the ground. It was the WWOOFers' job to break the limbs down and create piles for future burning. Dragging tree limbs across fields and pulling them apart by holding one piece down with your foot while ripping another part off with your hands—yes—that is what I call lumberjacking.

We all had scratches and bruises on our bodies at all times. No matter how careful I was, one of the limbs always found my leg or arm. Not to mention that nettle is the devil and yucca is its spawn. I constantly had fingers and toes go numb after rubbing against the nettle leaves, and the yuccas seemed to jump right out and prick me every chance they got.

On the bright side, taking down small trees by hand and pulling a mule cart completely eliminated the need for hand weights—you don't get this kind of workout in any gym. A fellow WWOOFer tagged a photo of me, "Mel, the mule," and she wasn't kidding. We literally pulled a mule cart full of branches and debris after an afternoon of lumberjacking.

Surprisingly, the repetitive manual disbanding of tree branches became enjoyable and, in many ways, liberating. Yes it was hard physical work but mentally it gave me a boost of confidence, and suddenly, I didn't feel helpless anymore. It was the first time I could remember in my adult life that I had no place I "had to be," except for where I was at that moment. Even if it was only for a small thing like manual lumberjacking, it allowed me to forget the fact that my life had just fallen apart and realize I was starting to gain some level of control over it. Not to mention the toning of my arms. It was a win-win.

There were lighter, less intense jobs as well, like weeding the vegetable garden or the Marie rose bushes. One job I volunteered for was mowing the château's lawn. The other WWOOFers were more than happy to forego this even though it was one of the easiest jobs there. The lawn was lush green grass that I got to cut with a gas-powered push mower—the only motorized piece of equipment we had. I love push mowing; I've been doing it since I was old enough to use a mower. It's great exercise, and the smell of fresh-cut grass is one of my favorite scents of life.

I also volunteered to weed and prune the raspberry patch, another task the other WWOOFers were happy to escape. They were another area of my expertise. There was a wild raspberry patch next to the vegetable garden of my child-hood home, and my mom and I picked gallons of berries each summer. We used to have raspberry cobbler year-round thanks to her. I admit I did not partake in deep patch activity as I was deathly afraid of snakes and always stuck to the perimeter that lined the driveway. Nonetheless, I did know how to dress for the occasion.

In Picardy, wearing protective layers of clothing was not a problem, and the tiny raspberry briars were completely irrel-evant. It was so bloody cold every morning I had to wear multiple layers of clothing to keep even a smidge warm. An entire suitcase full of clothes, yet I had not brought cold-weather clothing. Especially ones that were OK to work in and get dirty. I had one pair of jeans and one pair of leggings, both of which I wore together almost daily. I wouldn't start peeling off sweaters until around 10:00 a.m. and usually kept my leggings on throughout the day under my jeans. There were only a few hours a day that were warm and what I would consider "summer" clothing weather for most of my stay.

Cleaning—cleaning the house was often a challenge, both inside and out. It was weathered and fragile and I had to be careful not to break whatever I was cleaning. Like my friends the windowpanes. Rubbing too hard would cause pieces to break off—it would literally crumble into my hands. The same was true for the stairs and pavers outside. I had to remove the moss and weeds with a wire brush while trying not to damage them or chip pieces away. Not an easy task.

While we WWOOFers were always clean and sanitary with our cooking, the dishes were done in an odd fashion. It was the original kitchen with one small sink and no dishwasher. We would wash the dishes and either place them on a drying rack or most of the time, we hand dried and put the dishes away as we went. Again, this sounds rather normal, but there were two problems. When I first arrived I was told by the other WWOOFers that we only washed the dishes, we didn't rinse them. Wash and dry, no rinse. Yes, you are reading this correctly. So for the first ten days or so, that is how we did it. The second issue was the hand towels that we used to dry them. They didn't appear to get washed and reeked of mildew. You didn't have to worry about getting sick. All the antibodies to fight off infection were on the dishes.

I finally got the courage to ask Olivia about the lack of rinsing one day. Olivia was… how shall I put this nicely? A slightly loose cannon. In addition to her irritation over the language thing, she could be nice one second and flip out and scream at you the next over something minute. She wasn't exactly warm and fuzzy. But surprisingly, she thought it was as crazy as I did. It turns out that one of the WWOOFers had misunderstood her instructions and everyone was too afraid to ask.

One day, I had been tasked with creating floral centerpieces for the upcoming festival, and I apparently picked the wrong flowers. When she saw them, she began screaming and grabbed them from me and threw them all away. She had a complete meltdown—in full English—which I interpreted to be the equivalent of using someone's middle name to let them know they were in real trouble. Even making a salad could be nerve-racking. You had to cut the center of the romaine lettuce off; only the green leaf was to be eaten, but not the center. It was like helping out when you're home for the holidays with your family, and you can't seem to do anything the "right" way.

As temperamental as Olivia was though, she took extremely good care of us. The bedrooms and bathrooms were spotless; she would do all of our laundry, and we always had plenty of delicious food to cook and wine to drink. She also gave us the same day off so that we could all do something together as a group. She was nice in her own way and had good intentions.

In the end, all of our hard work for the festival paid off and it was a success. By festival day, the château and grounds looked pristine. Of course, none of the guests knew or could appreciate the level of prep work that had gone into it, but I did and that is what mattered.

# THE WWOOF DEN
## "Nightlife" at Picardy

By the end of my day, I just wanted to crawl into bed, get under the covers, and feel my toes again. Accommodations and amenities varied as much as the weather and were often much more interesting than the "nightlife."

Every evening after dinner Olivia would turn on the TV to watch movies—surprisingly American movies in English. The nights were cold and the heat in the house wasn't used. I can't blame her; it would have cost a small fortune. So when deciding whether to partake in movie night or make a heat cocoon in my bed, I opted for bed. I had my own room on the second floor of the château with my own bathroom, complete with a hot-water shower. I was sooooo grateful to have warm covers and a nightly hot shower. Had I not had them, I'm not sure I would have lasted two weeks. It was cold as hell at night.

Although my room there was unheated, it was my favorite WWOOFing accommodation for ambiance. The bedroom was like an antique boudoir. It had an alcove bed with a mini door on the side for changing the sheets. There were curtains on each side of the alcove front that could be closed or pulled back; the tick mattress and pillow were the original.

Even though the bed and bedroom were small compared to the palaces and enormous châteaus of French royalty's past, they provided a glimpse into the life of splendor. I envisioned retiring to my room at the end of my social-ite-filled day, my chambermaid taking my robe and turning down my bed as I put on my face cream and brushed my hair, preparing for a late evening visit from my handsome and powerful duke of a husband… Then my frozen toes and fingers brought me back to reality, and I realized I was cold, alone, and ready for night-night.

## BREAD CLEANED PLATES
### Feeding the WWOOF Pack

I didn't need to lick my plate; I simply wiped it clean with my baguette. I'm sure this one will come as no surprise to you—the food in France was outstanding. I did not have one bad meal *anywhere*. A "bread-cleaned plate" was the coolest cultural tradition I experienced, both for its literal meaning and symbolism. It is considered the norm to clean your plate with your bread when you have finished your meal. This went for both eating at home and at restaurants. Being a total foodie, this was just plain awesome.

There were four staples I consumed every day of my entire journey: cheese, bread, fresh veggies (usually spinach), and red wine. Every day, without exception. And one didn't ever need to worry about finding bread. Just like the wine and cheese, it was as delectable and accessible as water. Who would imagine that having a deliveryman could be so exciting? For the bread delivery, simply hang your bag out with the number of baguettes you want.

Blog post: *The Men of France*

*They have deliverymen here for the most important things: bread, meat, wine (yes, WINE)—they all deliver. That's right, folks. A wine man to your doorstep. However, one must bike to get milk. But then again, who needs milk if you have cabernet?*

As for WWOOFing, the meals varied at each location as to who, what, and how the meals were prepared. Sometimes the host would prepare meals and sometimes it was the WWOOFers' responsibility. A lot of the WWOOFers I met were vegetarians and extremely health-conscious. So most WWOOFing meals were vegetarian and the healthiest I've ever eaten. I only had meat a few times and it was usually in restaurants between WWOOFing locations. There was also barely little waste of food and everything else for that matter. Anything that was compostable was composted and most of our food was fresh from the garden, so the kitchen was eco-friendly throughout, and we usually consumed most of what we cooked that day.

WWOOFing mealtimes were mostly set in stone and were strictly adhered to at my WWOOFing locations. If breakfast time was 8:00 a.m., it meant 8:00, not 8:05. I was a little surprised to learn this considering how laid-back I had always thought Europeans were supposed to be concerning mealtimes. But I enjoyed having the structure and it took the guesswork out of it. The overall lunch and dinner mealtimes varied from location to location, as did the hosts joining you for meals. Some hosts never had meals with WWOOFers, some only had lunch or dinner, and some had all meals with us.

Nearly all breakfasts, including hotels, were as healthy as lunches and dinners. It was simply muesli cereal, bread, tea, unsweetened yogurt, and fruit. Notice that eggs are missing from this list. I love eggs and eat them every day at home. So breakfast without them was much more difficult to adjust to than no meat. Eventually I got used to it and didn't even notice they were absent from my life. The one thing I did miss however, was Typhoo, my favorite high-test, get-my-morning-started English tea. People there loved their coffee, but no one drank black tea; it was all green or herbal. I rejoiced whenever I would find Lipton at a hotel.

Since I was a WWOOFer, that meant I had to cook... ugh. I'm a mediocre cook. My mom was a phenomenal cook, but sadly it skipped a generation in my family. Most of my cooking skills were acquired from watching Food Network and that didn't happen until I was over thirty. I did alright though while I was there. No one got sick and I was never kicked out after a meal. I was pleasantly surprised when I managed to make a cucumber soup in Picardy that was quite tasty.

I was also extremely impressed at how well the younger WWOOFers could cook. Some of the best dinners of my life were prepared by them. Sarina made meals fit for royalty. She was not a professional but could easily be a world-renowned chef. She could make cardboard a five-star dinner. Some of the yummiest things she made for us were coq au vin, homemade gnocchi with garlic Alfredo sauce, and the Oscar winner food of my entire trip, acacia flower fritters.

I grew up in the country but had never heard of an acacia tree, much less eaten its blossoms. They resemble a miniature lilac with several tiny flowers nestled together to form a small bouquet. Sarina dipped them into a flour and egg batter and fried them in vegetable oil. Once fried, they were dipped in sugar immediately which allowed the sugar to caramelize. It was the most unique dessert I experienced in France.

Bon appétit!

## LES ARTISTES
## From Street to Church

Observing an artist at work is a magical experience. It doesn't matter who: painter, musician, sculptor. I'm not one who can sit down and draw a picture out of thin air or pick up an instrument and have beautiful music simply flow. Never have been. I believe musical talent, like cooking, skips a generation. My Dad could play multiple instruments, including the steel guitar. I can instantly detect a steel guitar in music pieces I hear, but that's the extent of my musical talent. So I'm always in awe of anyone who possesses a talent I do not. I can't comprehend how they do it and with such ease. Especially seeing them in person, their talent seems to ooze out of them.

Music was one of the many constants and was always present, in some form, all through my trip. Most of my WWOOFing adventures included concerts and WWOOFer recitals. I don't mean stadium-packed concerts, but smaller, more intimate ones. And they weren't hard to find. Summer music festivals and small concerts were common throughout the towns sprinkled across the country and impressively advertised. I saw paper flyers at almost all the cafés I went to.

Many WWOOFers played instruments and had brought them along, so there were often mini recitals happening during our siestas and days off. Sarina played the guitar in the afternoons before dinner.

During the festival at Olivia's, I went with her to an evening cello concert in the tiny little church next door. There wasn't a program, but Olivia thought it was Bach. Even though I am a fan of classical music, I can't recognize pieces by name so I had no idea. But it didn't matter. I would have still fallen in love with that concert regardless of the composer.

The cellist was from Paris, and he played for an hour and a half straight. The church was packed, and no one made a sound the entire performance. It was ninety minutes of mesmerizing and almost hypnotic sound. I think what astounded me the most was the purity, perfection, and smoothness. Every note flowed to the next and the small echo of the church carried it as if it were gliding from one angelic cloud to another. It created an immense feeling of inner peace inside me—one I hadn't felt in years and honestly, haven't felt on that level since. As I sat there, I imagined what it would be like to have lived back in the day of all the greats. Just imagine if your circle of friends included Bach or Chopin and you had the opportunity to attend a live performance at someone's dinner party. Imagine waltzing to Chopin across a friend's living room in your fluffy satin evening gown feeling like a princess. It is to this day, the most beautiful live music I've ever heard and my favorite concert of my life. I consider it one of my favorite French blessings.

I feel the same way about art as I do music. I love it and have a profound appreciation for the artists but I can't even draw a decent stick figure. While I have always loved art, my intrigue and deep curiosity about an artist's actual process began the year I met Steve Barton and William Dorsey in person and had the privilege of watching them paint right in front of me. I had never witnessed a professional artist at work before. It was like watching a beautiful flower bloom right in front of your eyes. In France I was fortunate enough to experience art at every turn and, luckily, managed to meet several artists in person.

I met Lucas Faytre while in Picardy. A lovely lady who does mostly sketches and watercolors. Olivia had commissioned her artwork for the exhibition at the château. She came to the château several days to work and would have lunch with us. She spoke some English and was happy to have someone to practice with.

As she walked the quiet streets of the tiny town, she carried her lawn chair and supplies and simply stopped wherever she found something she wanted to sketch. It was fascinating watching her choose a scene and quickly start to work. She ended up rolling out many beautiful watercolors to exhibit. We created a showroom in the game room of the château for the festival and hung her work on the walls surrounding the pool table. During the same week of the fete,

Lucas also had an exhibit at a middle school in Chantilly. Yes, as in the lace. She took all of us WWOOFers to the opening reception. It felt wonderful to witness her success and have her peers and fans acknowledge her talent.

On my last Sunday, I decided to attend the evening church service with Olivia in the same church as the cello concert. The service was Catholic and in French… so the joke was on God with that one. (I was raised Methodist, and I couldn't understand three words of the service.) Regardless, I did enjoy it and felt that God didn't care that I didn't understand; he was just happy to see me in church for once.

After the service ended, Olivia explained, in English, that the banner hanging on the wall was the church's original Saint-Jacques, Camino de Santiago banner. She told me the story of the Catholic Pilgrimage walk to Santiago, Spain, and how thousands of people would march each year. I had been so mesmerized by the Bach music during the concert that I hadn't taken notice of it.

It was overtly humbling to be sitting in a tiny little church in a tiny little country town, looking at its own tiny piece of history and soaking in the importance of one piece of fabric. That banner had been so paramount and prevalent. You could see its age, with its faded fabric and torn, fringed edges. Yet it had been carefully preserved and was so proudly hung. If only we would all maintain our convictions so strongly and consistently, imagine what we would accomplish—myself included.

## CHANTILLY LACE
### Raphael in the House

I absolutely loved the extreme convenience of trains all across the country. I did ninety percent of my travel by them and only had to take the bus a couple of times. I had never planned to drive while there and only regretted that once on my first attempt of getting to Giverny.

The trains were extremely convenient, clean, and on time, making day trips from my home bases a breeze. Even the rural countryside had trains, so it was usually easy to get to my destinations, usually... I had wanted to go visit Monet's home and gardens on my off day while I was in Picardy, but there was no service. I found out that going outward from a major city to a town was easy but hopping from town to town that were on different lines, was impossible. This would require me to go back to Paris to catch the train to Giverny, the same for the Champagne region. So Paris would become the hub for all of my northern excursions. Since I had already made a reservation in Reims for my lodging, I postponed Giverny until after Champagne, which I would visit immediately following my time in Picardy.

That didn't stop me from going on a day trip, however. Per Olivia's recommendation, I went to Chantilly. On my first trip there with Madame Faytre we had gone directly to the school and then straight back home. We had not seen any of the actual town center, so I decided it was an excellent choice. And I was right. Chantilly is the perfect day trip and another "must" for anyone spending time in or near Paris, with a small slice of everything you should experience when you visit France minus a vineyard. It's one of those places that I wouldn't mind going to over and over again to play tour guide for my friends and family. The main attractions were the château and the museum. It also had delicious macarons, three-cheese pizza, and great shopping. I do have to thank the weather for being responsible for a killer pair of jeans I found there. I had worn shorts and shocker... it was another cold, rainy day. I bought them in sheer desperation at Zoé Boutique in the center of town (still in business!) but ended up loving them.

The Château de Chantilly was my favorite château in France for art. It not only houses the Museé Condé, but also has a French formal garden, the Hameau de Chantilly, the Great Stables, and overlooks the Chantilly Racecourse. But it was raining and I spent most of my visit inside the château and museum.

The Museé Condé collection is only second to the Louvre in value and has a little something for everyone. Both the château and museum were bequeathed by the Duke d'Aumale to the Institut de France in 1897. But it did not come without conditions.[1] One of which was that the museum forbade the loaning of artworks to other institutions as well as insisting that the exhibition spaces not be modified in any way. As a result, the museum has remained almost unchanged since it was opened in 1898.

I admit I prefer Impressionism, but I could still appreciate and take in the magnitude of the art I was viewing. I had one moment which will always stand out in my art memory. When I looked at the Madonna of Loreto, I knew immediately it was a Raphael. I didn't need to read the nameplate, I knew. I distinctly remembered it from Ms. Poling's class. That was an exciting moment for me. I was more excited that I knew it was a Raphael than I was about actually seeing one. I can spot a Monet a mile away, but anyone else I wouldn't recognize by name. I impressed myself, which doesn't happen often.

# THE HOUSE OF KINGS
## Bring a Whiteboard

While the *Mona Lisa* is one of today's most famous and most visited ladies of France, Joan of Arc is certainly one of the most chivalrous, admirable, and heroic. I was privileged enough to visit Compiegne where she was captured by the Burgundians in 1430, and Rouen, where she died in 1431 at the hands of the British.

Compiegne was a journey in itself to get there and was my second day trip from Picardy. I biked to the local train stop, took the train to the Compiegne station, and biked to the edge of the village. That wasn't so bad; it was the fact that it took me forty-five minutes of walking around the perimeter of the village to realize all I had to do was simply walk directly straight ahead to get to the château and the center of town. *My lovely sense of direction had struck again.*

Olivia had told me that this was the village where Joan of Arc had been captured. What I didn't know until much later, was that it was also home to the Compiegne Forest,[2] where both World War Armistices had been signed.

The Armistice of WWI was in 1918 and WWII in 1940.[3] The Compiegne forest was chosen in 1918 to ensure secrecy from airplanes and journalists and security for the Germans from hostile French demonstrators.[4] The specific location was an old heavy artillery recoil pit that lay deep within the forest, now called the Armistice Clearing. Not only were both of the Armistices signed there, but they were also both signed in nearly identical fashion.[5] In 1918, the French had used a railway car which had once belonged to Napoleon III and was, at that time, General Foch's command wagon. ([6]General Foch was France's Commander-in-chief and military leader during the end of WWII.)[7] In 1940, Hitler demanded that the surrender be received in the exact same spot and in the exact same railway car. After which France remanded the car to Germany, where it was later destroyed and buried in Thuringia, Germany.

There was a memorial slab marking the location of the car at the Armistice Clearing, on view to the public six days a week. I did not see it the day I was there and it is one of my biggest regrets, both for not knowing it was there in the first place and not seeing the memorial. What an idiot, especially since it is in the forest next to the Château de Compiegne, where not only did I spend all afternoon walking around but was where Caesar had once won a battle. How exciting is that? Let this be another lesson for anyone who thinks history is not important, and when you own a Rick Steves book, use it. My next visit to Compiegne will be full of historical absorption.

The Château de Compiegne was the most overwhelming and largest château I visited. While I didn't take note of the size of every château and castle I toured, Château de Compiegne certainly looked the biggest. It has several "apartments" that have housed some of the most prominent royals of history's past. The list is long and contains multiple Napoleons, including [8]Napoleon I (his first date with Marie-Louise was here), King Louis XV, King Louis XVI, and Marie Antoinette.

Each room was large and over-the-top foo-foo. The entire château was full of statues, gold, extravagant fabrics, paintings, and on and on and on. It was all beautiful to look at and walk through, but for me personally less would certainly be more.

The foo-foo continued outside as well. The property covered nearly five acres and the grounds stretched on forever. There were gardens, parks, and a Central Park-like "backyard." The Avenue De Beaux-Monts is [2]nearly 5 kilometers long and sixty meters wide. Translated, that is almost two and a half miles long. The trees had been cleared by Napoleon I beginning in 1810 and were finished two years after his death in 1823. That's a lot of trees for manual lumberjacking.

When it came to Joan of Arc, however, the village wasn't screaming too loudly for her. I found a small statue and a hanging banner of her crest, but those were the only signs of her past I spotted. Not nearly as many as I had anticipated and certainly not as flamboyant as the château and

its history. I suppose the spotlight on the place she was captured is slightly dimmer than that of where she died.

# THE GLASS IS FULL
## Tasting Devil Wine

Blog Post: *Bubbles*

*"What would champagne be without the fizzing bubbles?*
*Wine... it would merely be wine."*

I understand that champagne is not for everyone. However,
after living in one of the most prominent wine countries of

the world, which is also the home of Champagne, I now realize that it is not a competition. It's more of a relationship. It's like dark and milk chocolate. They are vastly different, but yet equally delicious and important.

One of my few regrets was that I didn't spend more time in the Champagne region. I only spent a day and a half in Reims and for a champagne lover, it wasn't long enough. To put more salt in the wound, I found out that my favorite brand of champagne, Veuve Clicquot (at that time), was not open for general public tours. So I crossed it off my list and kept my schedule completely open and unplanned with the exception of my B&B reservation.

I am very proud to say that I only got lost *once* the entire trip and that was in Reims. I took the train from Paris coming straight from Picardy and walked to the B&B I thought I was staying at. You guessed it, I went to the wrong one. It was similar to how we have Beverly Street, Beverly Avenue, and Beverly Way. I was on the Street instead of the Avenue. Luckily, the owners spoke some English and were kind enough to get me in a taxi and tell the driver where I needed to go. They were an extremely sweet couple and looked about the right age that they could have been my parents. In some small way, I felt as if they were treating me like a friend of their daughter's who had come home to visit. It was comforting to have someone take care of me, even if only for a brief moment. Isn't it funny how kind gestures received from complete strangers that you can't even understand can comfort you?

This experience was a good travel lesson: always take a taxi when you arrive, and if it is easily walkable, walk back to the train when you're leaving. Especially when you are in a larger town or city. (*If only the ride-share apps had existed then.*)

On the plus side, the "tastings" in Reims are nothing like any tastings I had ever experienced. The champagne houses don't pour a few sips like you normally get at a vineyard tasting; *they pour full glasses.* I also loved that Reims is small enough to walk from house to house, so taxis aren't needed. That is, providing one can still walk after multiple full glass tastings… Reims was positively my happy place of France.

The tastings were not just about drinking the bubbly or learning the modern production process either. To France, champagne is part of its history. So learning about the history of champagne serves as a small French history lesson in itself. Several houses offered a tour of the caves and cellars, so you are literally going through some of the original caves of champagne's birthplace. My favorite tour was at Mumm because they also had a small museum onsite.

As I walked through the dimly lit caves, I pictured the monks wearing their heavy robes and holding candles to light their way down the narrow stairs. The heavy robes must have come in handy, as the caves are a bit chilly and I suspect, like a mine. I grew up a coal miner's daughter, but believe it or not, I've never stepped foot inside one. So I can only imagine that they are similar. Of course, this would be the only similarity. A monk's day at the office was a heck of a lot safer than a miner's. At least after the eighteenth century that is, when the bottling and corking requirements of sparkling wine began to be understood.

In the early years, before advanced champagne technology, the bottles would often spontaneously explode and injure the cellar workers. [10]They had to wear iron masks to protect themselves. The unexplained sparkling, explosion wine was often referred to as [11]"The Devil's Wine." Talk about an occupational hazard!

As with any invention, there is often controversy surrounding the "first" of something. Champagne is no different. Even naming the stuff was controversial. Supposedly, the first champagne was accidentally invented by monks in southern France near Carcassonne well before the northern champagne era began. Regardless of the real father of champagne, it has been produced in the Champagne region of France for most of its adult life. As for naming one's sparkling devil wine "champagne," that can be a tad tricky. There is probably a lawbook written on the subject, as the protection of the name "champagne" has been in play since the 1800s. As a general rule, most labeling only uses "champagne" for the sparkling wines that actually come from the Champagne region of France.

The original bottling equipment and production lines were as engrossing as the caves and history themselves. From the basket-chain system to the corking machine, I was amazed at how much of the old equipment was on display. Not to mention the old bottles of champagne still sitting there waiting to be popped, with years of dust still on them. It was like walking through a historical episode of *How It's Made*.

## STANDING IN THE FOOTSTEPS
## A Front-Row Seat to History

The wonderful part of truly discovering history for the first time was that I didn't have to be a history buff to appreciate it nor to be completely mesmerized by it. I expected to learn *some* history in France; after all, the entire continent of Europe is like a giant history book. But I had no idea the substantial amount I would actually learn and experience in person, nor the emotional influence it would have on me.

I hated history in school. It was so boring at the time and often torturous reading. None of the characters ever came to life for me and I had no interest at all, so I didn't have any French historical items on my entire must-see list. However, experiencing it in person quickly reversed my viewpoint, something I had not anticipated as most of my favorite history morsels were stumbled upon by accident. Some were while WWOOFing, others while playing tourist. But I never had to travel far from my base camps to find them.

Even if I had planned and researched things to do, nothing could have prepared me for the emotions and feelings I experienced when I was literally standing in the footsteps of history. It's like when you are asked one of those questions that you can't answer because the answer only comes when you're actually in that moment. When the realization hit me that I was walking where some of the most influential people to ever exist once walked, there were no words to thoroughly describe the feelings. I found a new level of respect for history I didn't know was possible. I was honored and grateful to have had the privilege of seeing firsthand where historical moments took place. No history class could ever teach those experiences.

The Room of Surrender in Reims is one of them. I read about it in my Rick Steves guide on the train ride from Paris and decided to include it on my Reims champagne self-guided tour. [12]On May 7, 1945, Germany's Third Reich unconditionally surrendered to the Allied forces, ending World War II and halted what most of us consider the worst genocide in modern history. They did so at what was then General Eisenhower's supreme headquarters in Reims, which is now a museum.

The Salle de la Signature room had been part of Reims's technical college and was kept intact, just as it was on that day. The room was small, especially considering the magnitude of its significance. Maps of Europe covered the walls, and it felt as if they were constricting and overpowering everything inside. The wooden rectangular table surrounded by simple wooden chairs sat in the middle and took up most of the room. I slowly absorbed that I was standing in the very room where WWII ended and was breathing in the air that once changed the world forever.

As I stood there, I pictured the room full of generals and high-ranking soldiers ensconced together around the table as the session kicked off. The air, paralyzingly thick with stress and anxiety, while they wrestled with the weight of the world on their shoulders. The overwhelming sense of relief, patronage, and benevolence after the German Instrument of Surrender was signed and the war was officially over. The collective exhaustion, anger, and animosity encompassing the lives lost from the horror and the lives to be spared from the surrender; a lot of emotions for one small room.

I left the museum that day with feelings of honor, respect, and humaneness. It was undoubtedly one of those times when I needed a few minutes afterward to fully comprehend what I had just experienced and to let the magnitude of importance sink in. I was grateful to be next to the champagne caves, I certainly needed a drink after that one, or perhaps some chocolate mousse. There was also the prayer route as churches continued to pop up. – I of course, opted for the champagne alternative (as my Aunt Peg prays for better choices in my future.)

# JE SUIS UN TOURISTE
## Yeah, I've Been There

The weather was finally getting a little warmer as I made my way back to Paris for a one-and-a-half-day tour, *and it wasn't raining!* I wanted to see as much as possible of the city before my next stint, so first up was my rooftop-bar excursion to the Hotel Raphael. It was luxurious and posh, as if I had walked into the New York Waldorf Astoria of Paris. The concierge escorted me to the elevator and the bellboy took me up to the bar. I was there in the early afternoon and had the place all to myself. I felt like I was in *Pretty Woman*—but without the hot, rich guy buying my drink. The views were as spectacular as the service. The Eiffel Tower is on one side and the Arc de Triomphe on the other. It was, and still is, my favorite view of Paris.

In my broken French, I asked the waiter to take my picture with the Eiffel Tower in the background. A few sips of red later, while I was admiring the gorgeous view, I realized that I *was* doing something with my life. I was out there making something happen. It may have only been simply getting myself to my dream country and having a glass of fine French wine while overlooking one of the most iconic structures of the world, but it was something. I was moving forward. It was one of those moments that gave me the gumption to keep going. Scared or not, I was living out one of my dreams. And what a perfect setting for such a realization too. It was just me, Paris, and a glass of smooth red wine. I couldn't have asked for a better experience. Well… maybe the hot, rich guy.

I managed to find quite a bit on my list that afternoon. I'm rather good at seeing a "City in a Day," and I had a lot to pack in as I was going to Giverny next.

Art lover or not, one could not step foot into Paris without going to the Louvre. It's a rite of passage for visiting the city. Sadly, however, it was disappointing for me. It was so crowded and time-consuming to maneuver myself around. The layout required you to walk through multiple sections with no options of weaving in and out or up and down. It's like the grocery store trick of putting the milk in the back. It took me two hours to reach the *Mona Lisa* and *Monsieur de Milo*. I didn't have the patience to fight the crowds any longer, exploring the streets of Paris was much more exciting.

The Odeon, Berkely Books, and a chocolate croissant topped off the day's experience.

# WATER LILY TEARS
## A Day of Gratitude

Giverny was one of the main reasons I chose France as my WWOOFing destination and I had nearly exploded when I found out about the Impressionism Festival that covered the entire Normandy region. But what I hadn't thought about was what my experience would be like once I actually got to Monet's home.

I had never been subjected to a true pilgrimage before, nor did I fully understand the significance and effect one could have on a person; I had simply read about them, along with the recent Picardy story. So needless to say, I didn't realize I was on one of my own until I arrived in Giverny and was standing in front of Monet's water garden.

Gazing across the pond at the Japanese bridge, the water lilies, and weeping willows, knowing this was where some of the world's most precious paintings were created soaked deep into the core of my soul and brought tears to my eyes. It was a magical experience, I felt like I was walking in one of his paintings. I could visualize him sitting there with his canvas and paintbrush, alone in the early morning, wisping together a masterpiece as if it were just another Tuesday. I wondered if he had known in his heart that his work would turn into some of the most prestigious paintings to ever grace us or if he simply looked at his work as doing what he loved to do. Either way, it must have been a pure blessing for him. Making a living doing what you love is, to many of us, only a fantasy.

I spent most of my time at Giverny walking through the gardens. Primarily because that was the setting for much of his work that I love, and the house tour was so packed and the lines so long, I opted to experience the outdoors. I was soaking in the amazement I felt and my overall appreciation for being there. I didn't want to pollute that with chatty tourists and white noise. As I walked, I felt as if I was conveying a private expression of gratitude to him and kept to myself.

All the gardens were breathtaking. From the nymphs in the pond to the gardens by the house, every color you could imagine was there. It was the epitome of horticulture precision. It looked as if there wasn't a blade of grass, nor flower petal out of place. Absolute gorgeous, garden perfection.

The icing on the Giverny cake was the Musée des Impressionnismes, which was only a short walk from Monet's home, so I stopped there on my way back to the train station. There were other artists exhibited of course, but to look at a Monet right after leaving his house was almost surreal. In fact, I can't even tell you any of the other artists displayed. I was on cloud nine and had no sense of reality. I was living in a Monet movie.

## ROYAL SECRETS
## The Unplanned Treasures

The history lessons continued in Amboise, a small Loire Valley town that sits by the Loire River. It's quaint, cheery, and small enough to tour in a few hours. But because I was between my Picardy and Parthenay WWOOFing locations and I had already booked my room, I spent the night anyway. And I was happy to take a break and prepare myself for the next adventure. After all, I was there to embrace the country, and Amboise felt like the perfect place to absorb more French culture and recharge.

Other than my hotel, I had made no plans and began my spontaneous tour d'Amboise at the Château Royal d'Amboise. It had been the home to many royal families (including multiple Louis), some of whom used it only as a part-time residence. You know—a little house in the country to get away from it all.[13] Sometimes, it would be to house the wife and kids while the king entertained his mistress elsewhere. *No further comment.*

The high-ceilinged Gothic-style château was beautiful and full of carved wooden furniture and large tapestries hung on the walls. Some rooms were more colorful than others, but nothing like I had seen at Chantilly. They were large and timelessly sophisticated but didn't have gold plastered everywhere nor extravagant trim moldings. The intricate detail and magnificence was in the architecture. The Great Hall on the main floor was full of flawlessly curved arbor archways that gracefully cascaded from one to another along the length of the room.

As beautiful as the château was—and I certainly wouldn't refuse to live there—I was more impressed with the spectacular panoramic Loire Valley views. The château was set on the Loire riverbank and had luscious green lawns on the opposite side with wide dirt paths that wound through the surrounding grounds. The views were fabulous yet at the same time, a tad intimidating. It was difficult to imagine seeing them if they were from my own living room. One of those moments when I couldn't wrap my head around the beauty and the wealth.

Even more impressive was that the château had its own church right next door, the Chapel of Saint-Hubert. It is small in size but had as much, if not more, Gothic architectural design as the château, both inside and out. The carvings on the exterior were mind-blowing with such intricate detail and beauty of perfectly carved human figures, animals, and tiny trees. I doubt I will ever understand how carvings and sculptures are created, especially in that time period. The interior was full of gorgeous design with the same arbor archways as the château, as well as gorgeous stained glass. Its most precious attribute, however, was that it was where Leonardo da Vinci rests. For me, the beauty & size ratio makes it the most beautiful church I've ever been in. It's the best chapel for your tourist buck in France.

Back in the 1500s, the Château Royal was home to King Francis I. It was during his stay that Leonardo moved into the Clos Luce, a nearby château. The legend goes that the king and Leonardo used the underground tunnel that connected both châteaus to go back and forth, allowing them to avoid their version of the paparazzi. Apparently, château tunnels were once common. The château I stayed at in Picardy had one too, which led to the château next door (although no one uses it anymore.)

As a tourist bonus of the Château Royal, there was a fun tasting room at the bottom of the hill. It was a mixture between a wine bar and a tasting room. This was my first official wine tasting in France and the wines were delicious! But unfortunately they didn't ship and quickly became another *suitcase moment.

As I was leaving the tasting room, I noticed many small groups of people walking down the road and they looked like they knew where they were going. I was afraid I might be missing something, so I decided to follow them. We ended up at the Clos Luce. Of course... how did I not figure that one out? So only minutes after visiting the grave of Leonardo, I was touring his home and gardens. *Yes, this was*

*in my Rick Steves guide, but I had not paid attention to the
Amboise details. Even though I was having the best time of my
life at that stage, I was just too exhausted to plan adventures.*

Now by château standards, Clos Luce is on the smaller
side yet was my favorite château I toured. Perhaps the small
size was why it was my favorite. Or maybe it was because it
was so perfectly decorated, *or* perhaps simply because I had
just completed a generously poured wine tasting.

In truth, I think it was because as I walked through, it
felt like someone still lived there. It was simplistically regal:
somewhat fancy and picture-perfect, yet homey and comfortable all at the same time. Unlike so many of the over-the-top
châteaus I had visited, the ceilings weren't fifteen feet tall and
gold was not the primary décor staple. It was realistic, relat-
able, and simply felt more down-to-earth and welcoming.

There were several rooms open to the public, and the
kitchen, by far, was the most interesting. I believe it housed
every size and shape of copper pots in the history of copper
cookware. If the dinner parties thrown for the royal family
while Leonardo lived there were anything like the kitchen,
they would have been idyllic. I could almost smell the coq
au vin roasting in the oven.

There was a group of children there on what looked
like a field trip. They had worksheets and were writing and

chatting away as they sat on the floor of one of the rooms inside. Imagine being eight years old and your field trip is to Leonardo da Vinci's house. How awesome would that be? I can't even begin to relate.

As much as I loved the kitchen, it could not compare to the historical awesomeness of the master bedroom. Standing next to the bed where one of the most influential men of mankind used to sleep was one of my favorite *awe* moments of my trip. I had recently seen the *Mona Lisa* at the Louvre and now, there I was, standing in the bedroom of the artist who painted it. It might have even hung there at one time. Another indescribable experience.

The outdoor gardens were as beautiful as the inside. Everything was meticulously manicured. Gorgeous flowers and plants surrounded by perfectly groomed grass outlined his numerous inventions placed throughout the property. It was far from a starving artist's studio.

I once again left a historical location with feelings of humility and gratitude. I was so thankful that da Vinci got to experience some of his success and live the way an artist should, unlike van Gogh and so many others. I was thrilled I went to Amboise and learned more about him. Another unplanned and unexpected treasure. *I absolutely love those.*

*Oh that suitcase. The darn thing ended up busting at the seams as I made my way to my hotel and I had to buy a new one. Amboise is a touristy town with shops lining the streets, including, conveniently enough, a luggage store. I opted for a smaller version, which meant no wine in the suitcase. I didn't think that one through too well... If only I had bought the suitcase *after* my tour. Another travel lesson learned the hard way.

# I KNOW WHERE I'M GOING
## Oui, à Gauche

By this time, I had learned—okay, partially grasp—how to ask for directions, albeit broken, but I could get my question across well enough to make do. I could confidently ask, "Where is [blank]?" and desperately grasp onto any words I could understand from someone's response and begin the charade language game. Usually a few hand gestures and pointing fingers combined with one or two translated words got me where I was going. For example, if the answer was, "Go straight for three blocks, then turn left," the person would usually hold up three fingers and say, "à gauche" (turn left) somewhere in their response. After I had solved the direction puzzles a few times, that was generally all I needed.

However… there were times this technique didn't work out quite so well. It was extremely difficult at bus stations. I nearly missed the bus to Parthenay simply because they didn't post the gate numbers and I couldn't understand what anyone was saying to me to save my life. I showed my ticket to one of the transit workers and she ended up sprinting me to the gate as the bus was pulling out. It was like a commercial; I just made it. Bless those French I tell you!

# PARTHENAY
## A Soul-Soother

Parthenay is a medieval city in the middle of Western France, about one and a half hours northeast of La Rochelle. It is large enough to be a city, but small enough to have that small-town feel. It was a short drive to the beach, it had all the modern conveniences and bonus—there was a golf course nearby. I didn't have an opportunity to play, but just knowing there was one made it feel homey.

I was WWOOFing for a single woman named Simone. She was a schoolteacher and lived in a modest house in a subdivision of the town with a large enough yard with maintenance requirements that she was unable to keep up with alone. I was the sole WWOOFer and stayed one week. But boy, did we fit a lot in.

Simone spoke English, and was compassionate to use it, yet I always remember my time there when I think of my "dictionary conversations." These conversations were with complete strangers and are some of my fondest language memories. They are also a superb sampling of how friendly, funny, and welcoming I found the French people to be. On my first day, she dropped me off at La Rochelle Beach while she went to her nearby *Eskrima-type martial arts lesson. This was going to be my first French beach and I was excited! *Mostly because it would be the first time since I left New York City that I would be able to feel my toes.*

Luckily La Rochelle was warm enough that day to sunbathe and I wasted no time. My first observation was that the beach wasn't full of topless women. I was used to going topless in Saint Martin and assumed it would be the same here. I had been looking forward to no tan lines but was so grateful to have sunshine I didn't even care. The beach itself wasn't touristy and overly crowded; it had a subdued family vibe full of quiet, happy, tanning people. A perfect beach day for relaxing, warming my bones, and soaking in the French rays.

I bathed for a few hours but eventually became a little unsettled and anxious. This was week number three into my trip and I was still acclimating to my vagabond life and never knowing what to expect from day to day. The unknowns were often scary and I still felt lost within my own life on a daily basis. The flip side of vagabonding though, is it allows each day to be a new adventure. But I still wasn't used to the freedom I was experiencing and wasn't sure if the 'new adventures' were going to continue to be positive ones. I needed to move around a little to settle my nerves. So I set off to explore and calm my jitters.

The beach had a beautiful walking path that stretched all along the beach's edge. I walked for several minutes, found a bench, and sat down to listen to the sounds of the waves crashing to decompress.

As I breathed in the salty air of freedom, a lovely older lady sat down next to me. We both smiled and she said something in French, a pleasantry I'm sure, but of course, I didn't understand a word. I gave my tried and true "*Je parle Anglais,*" and she laughed and replied back with something that I determined meant she only spoke French. We ended up having a great conversation. And by "conversation" I mean six to ten sentences that took twenty minutes for us to translate with each other using my dictionary. We laughed the entire time because, to us, it was a comedy. I don't even remember what we talked about. My memory is of the fun we had and the laughter we shared. She was a beautiful lady, both inside and out. That afternoon was a soul-soother and gave me confidence that I would be OK for the remainder of my trip and that I would in fact, be able to get by without speaking the language.

The next day Simone took me to a festival at the Château d'Oiron in Plaine-et-Vallées, another 45-minute drive from her home. The small village had blocked off the streets and there were at least a dozen spots with different types of music and dancing surrounding the château. Château d'Oiron wasn't furnished or fancily decorated like the others I visited. It had various artwork displayed throughout and was set up like an art gallery that day. We met up with a group of Simone's friends who had their own singing group. Before we knew it, they had all formed a circle around us and had us sit on the ground while they sang to us. It was our own personal concert serenade. I felt like we were the most important people on the grounds that day, the VIPs of d'Oiron.

I had another language comedy during my stay here. I saw one of my all-time favorite foreign films that week with Simone. One evening we decided to have dinner and a movie night at home. She had the DVD *Saint-Jacques La Mecque* by Coline Serreau and she thought I would enjoy it. It was in French of course and had no subtitles. She explained in English the storyline and the characters. It was about siblings who were required to go on a pilgrimage together in order to get their inheritance. That's all I knew—and then we pushed Play. I watched the entire movie and probably only understood maybe six words—not exaggerating. Yet it was one of the funniest, most well-acted movies I've ever seen. The beautiful part was I didn't need to understand the dialogue to understand the scenes. The expressions, gestures, voice inflections, and overall delivery said it all. The movie was superb.

School was still in session while I was there, so most days I was home alone, alongside the dog, cat, and chickens. I was so happy to be by myself and had not been since Paris. Not to mention that I had had roommates since my divorce, so I was loving every minute of my alone time. I have always loved it, even as a child, so for me it was wonderful. Although I can't really say I did a lot of soul-searching during that week. I was still avoiding the fact that my life, once I returned home, would still be in shambles. So, I stepped away from reality and lived in the moment as if life were perfect. After all, I was living my French dream.

*Eskrima is a Filipino martial art that uses sticks, knives, and empty-hand techniques for self-defense. Simone used a long stick that looked like a large cricket racket.

# CHICKENS AND CHEESE
## It's All Recyclable

Simone cooked most of the dinners except for the one night when I made her penne with vodka sauce and garlic bread, which surprisingly she loved. I had mentioned my love of cheese to Simone shortly after my arrival, so she surprised me one evening with an entire cheese buffet she bought at the market. Our tasting was comprised of four hard cheeses and a cheese "cake." The cake was black on top (burnt, to be precise) and wasn't sweet like dessert cheesecake. It had the texture and consistency of a heavy cornbread. That evening felt like a cheese birthday party and is one of my favorite "foodie" memories.

I was grateful that each WWOOFing location had a slightly different cheese palette, so there were always new ones to try. And I easily tried at least thirty different cheeses during my four months. At least I think I did… After a while, all the labels looked alike and I of course could barely read them, but regardless I loved them all.

All of my work at Simone's was outside in the yard. Yes, you guessed it… weeding and trimming trees. But the mule cart and dull tools in Picardy were a stark contrast to the large trailer and modern tools I had to work with here. While still back-aching work, the sharp tools allowed me to actually see the fruit of my labor within hours instead of days. I put all the yard clippings and debris into the trailer, which hooked up to her van, so all I had to do was load the trailer—once. Now I still did some lumberjacking, but it was on a lighter, more productive scale. I actually saw the light at the end of the tunnel before I even started.

Simone had a rooster and a few hens that had reigned over the entire backyard. They would assist me with raking the back pathways after I had cleared them. I would put the leaves into the wheelbarrow to dump behind the fence, and they would jump on top of the pile and dig for food. They were like cats insisting they lie on your wrapping paper during gift wrapping.

The entire yard needed work, so I would start at one end and work my way around. That system allowed me to mix it up and not do the same task all day. I would trim branches for a couple of hours, then switch to weeding or raking. That method also helped with my back pain. I would work six or seven hours each day with a short break at noon to make my own lunch, which consisted of some leftovers from the previous night's dinner or a simple plate of bread and cheese buffet.

Most afternoons after finishing the day's tasks, I would walk into town to explore. I went through both residential areas and the town center, taking a different street each time. I wanted to experience as much as I could and I believe you see more when you are walking as opposed to driving or riding a bike. The suburbia community looked like any other apart from the cars in the driveways.

The negative thing I discovered about walking was going past house gates along the sidewalk. The driveways were gated on over half the houses, and the gates were solid with a four-inch gap at the bottom and as I walked past the gate, the family dogs would bark, growl, and stick their noses from under it scaring me to death. I would jump and scream every time. It took a couple of days to remember to expect the loud and obnoxious barking. I love dogs, but that was annoying as hell, especially considering they sounded like they wanted to tear my leg off.

After a week of tree trimming and weeding, I had accumulated various piles of debris and branches around the yard. Unlike being in the country at Olivia's where she would either burn the branches or save them for firewood, Simone was in the "city" and we had to haul everything for disposal. So the day before I left, Simone and I hitched the trailer to her van and loaded it up. I did a little dance on top of the pile to make room for more until we had it packed to the brim and we were off to the local recycling center to dump it.

While going to a recycling center might not sound enticing, I was anxious to see it. This was the kind of experience I wanted to have: an inside look at everyday life in France and the opportunity to understand just how similar we all live. Did they separate plastic from glass? Were the newspapers tied together or flying all over the place? I wanted to research this important environmental information.

It turned out, the center was similar to ours. You show proof of residency and drive around to the appropriate dumpster. They had one for each item, so they did in fact separate. We emptied the trailer rather quickly and were on our way. My conclusion on the recycling side of life—recycling is recycling.

## LE MARCHÉ
# I Ask for It

One of the many elements of France that I was looking forward to the most was the markets. I was curious to see what they offered and couldn't wait to experience them. To me, a market reflects the core lifeline of a community and culture that flows through the arteries of local life. It defines the lifestyle, culinary staples, and an overall sense of attitude toward healthy choices. I was used to the farmers' and flea markets in New York City and antique markets of New Jersey, but I didn't know what to expect in France other than lots of fresh lavender. I was fortunate enough to visit different kinds at various locations while I was there and loved them all for their individual flair, products, and ambiance. The markets, as it turned out, have a culture all their own.

I discovered three types: farmers', flea, and town square markets. If you are into markets and go to any town in France that has one (regardless of the market size), do yourself a solid and set aside time for the exploration. You will learn more in one day about the people and the culture at the market than a week at museums and touristy shops.

In fact, one glimpse can sometimes say everything. I learned early on in Parthenay to remember that I was in France and to not be surprised at what I might find while shopping at the market. The brain was a bit more than I bargained for, but after all, it was one of the magnificent cultural experiences I was so desperate to find. As the cliché goes, be careful what you wish for.

## A REAL FRENCH BREAKFAST
## Saint-Jacques Would Be Proud

My last full day with Simone was a Saturday and full of treats. First, she introduced me to a traditional "French Breakfast," which by most standards did not fall into that healthy breakfast category I was growing accustomed to. It consisted of buttered bread (fresh bread made that morning) slathered in fresh butter and dunked into hot chocolate (the real kind made with milk and cocoa). So simple yet so incredibly delish. It was pure morning bliss and by far my favorite calorie-bomb breakfast.

Afterward, she treated me to a three-and-a-half-hour tour of the city while explaining things in a fun, storytelling way. I'm sure her students love her; the way she empowers you to enjoy yourself while soaking up the historical details without falling asleep or wanting to jump off of a castle wall. If only she had been my History teacher, I would have been a historian genius.

The entire city felt like a movie set. I'm sure lots of places in Europe look that way. But this was my first medieval city, and like with my first château, it immediately lured me in.

As we walked the spotless winding streets, Simone educated me on the city's rich history including how it is in the middle of the Santiago route. Parthenay was like a fortress that still has its bridges and large sections of its castle walls in place, complete with lookout windows that at one time had been the village's eyes to the world. I was impressed with their design and construction. The six-inch opening allowed one to gaze miles into the city. As I rubbed my hand over the cool, rough stone, I envisioned the soldiers decked out in their shiny armor, patrolling the castle walls, looking out to spot enemy armies approaching. It was exhilarating to know my hand was resting on the same spot where medieval soldiers once rested theirs. This view was one of my trip's favorites.

Homes were built atop the castle wall. I was overwhelmed just by walking around, and I can't imagine what it would be like to actually live there. How cool it must be for children to grow up playing soldier at a *real* castle.

As the walking history tour continued, she explained the significance of the scallop shell I kept seeing everywhere. It was the Saint-Jacques shell and played a large role in the pilgrimage. The homeowners hung the shell above their front door to signal to the pilgrims that they were welcome into that home while passing through on their journey. Knowing I was walking on the same path that so many had walked before, the very path that the Picardy church's banner had been carried, felt quietly surreal. I felt more and more like I was a pop-up figure in a history book. Not surprisingly, the Saint-Jacques shell still holds its symbolic stature today. You can even find shell pastries in the supermarche, testimony to the importance of culture throughout France and their impressive conviction for preservation.

Simone also taught me a fun fact about the meaning of street names and how you can unravel the history of a town just by reading them. Like Rue de la Vau-Saint-Jacques, which had been the main street of the pilgrimage in Parthenay. I had never really thought about street names until that moment. Isn't it funny how such simple little things in front of us every day go unnoticed? I now find myself consciously looking at street names and piecing together a little story for that section of town, like envisioning the lemon harvests on Lemon Grove Lane.

# TORSAC
## Pillow, Please

Nestled in the Poitou-Charentes region, Torsac is the quintessential example of French country charm. The surrounding towns are small but pristine and it was home to the best homemade pâté of my life. Even though it was only thirty-five miles from Cognac, I never made it over for a tasting. There wasn't a lot of downtime and I'm not a big brandy fan anyway, so it made no difference to me. Maybe next time.

I had chosen the Torsac host location because the Printemps Chapiteau Theater Festival was going to be held while I was there and I wanted to meet some French actors. This was also my longest WWOOFing stay, I spent nearly three weeks there, but it certainly didn't seem like it. I had so much fun and met some of the most talented people! I would have stayed longer if my schedule had permitted.

My hosts were Marq and Paige. I knew immediately upon meeting them when they picked me up at the bus stop, that I would love them when I answered, "No" to their first question to me of, "Do you speak French?" Both were so kind. Paige responded with, "I will teach you." Marq's response was, "We will help you learn," both in perfect English. Relieved, I knew the French lessons were going to be more enjoyable as I made my way through my scheduled WWOOFing locations. Thank goodness.

While they were technically not farmers, their garden was several acres and had any vegetable you could possibly want. They also had a small greenhouse where they planted their own seedlings and a covered area of the garden for starting the small plants.

There were six of us WWOOFers during most of my stay and we were never short on work. One of the WWOOFers, Cadence, was in her sixties and French-Canadian. I had great respect for her. She had just retired and wanted to travel the world and WWOOFing was allowing her to do so. I quickly became conscious that the French can detect an American accent from a mile away. French-Canadian accents too for that matter and they don't hesitate to call it out. Cadence got the brunt of the ball-busting. I did not go unscathed, however. I was corrected more than once—but always in a fun, help-me-to-learn kind of way.

I shared a room with her, also unheated like Picardy and a theme of WWOOfing I guessed. It was across the driveway from the main house, where the kitchen, bathroom, and showers were located.

On my first night, I had gone to my room to turn in and saw that I didn't have a pillow. So my dictionary and I went back into the main living room to ask Paige for one. I knew how to say, "I would like [blank] please," so all I had to do was add 'pillow.' But for the life of me, no one could understand me. I knew it was the correct word because I was reading straight from the page. I repeated myself several times and finally had to ask in English. They all had a good laugh once they knew what I was trying to say. But at least I had made the effort and they appreciated it.

With nighttime, comes the occasional trip to the bath-room. While most of my nightly bathroom adventures throughout my journey were uneventful, there were a couple in Torsac when avoiding going to the bathroom in the middle of the night was not an option. The weather in Torsac was the coldest I experienced. It nearly snowed one night—*in June.*

On two different nights, I woke up at 3:00 a.m. with those atomic stomach cramps. You know the ones when you have approximately five minutes to get to where you're going. I would quietly get out of bed, layer up, put on my sneakers, and grab the flashlight. There were several dogs in the area, so I had to dodge the poop on the path as well as maneuver the stairs up to the back of the house. I barely made it in time both nights and luckily no embarrassing moments.

# DON'T WAKE THE GROUNDHOG
## It's a Circus Here

Our WWOOFing assignments initially began with a couple days' worth of weeding and gardening, true to WWOOFing form. This was where I met a very special friend. One morning Sydney, another WWOOFer, and I were replanting seedlings when he uncovered a sleeping groundhog. I saw groundhogs all the time growing up, but I had never been that up close and personal with one. Luckily it didn't wake up! We simply tucked it back in and dug a couple of feet away.

Sydney was an experienced WWOOFer and probably ten years younger. He was from Paris but spoke excellent English. As I got to know him during my stay, it became apparent that he was mainly interested in farming and was the complete opposite of me. He was raised in the city but was a country boy at heart. Sydney was a solid gentleman through and through, one of those people that you instinctively know it's okay to give your house key to.

What I hadn't realized when I confirmed with Marq and Paige was that they were the festival's caterer, so for the remainder of my stay catering was our sole focus. Two days before the festival was to begin, we were all assigned to pre-festival preparedness. Part of that prep work consisted of spending an entire day cleaning the kitchen and dining room from top to bottom in preparation for cooking and serving. The main house used to be a B&B with a small restaurant and the layout was like a lodge. The kitchen, dining, and sitting areas were all open, with a fireplace at the end. And since it used to be a restaurant, the kitchen was catering friendly and was the perfect spot to cater a small festival.

This also meant there was *a lot* to clean, and we cleaned *every square inch*. Behind the stove, behind the refrigerator, under the sink, all the cabinets, the pantry—the entire thing. It was white glove-ready by the time we went to bed that night. The best part—that was my favorite WWOOFing day. Cleaning is my favorite chore and I was thrilled to not be in the garden or weeding. There was a lot of standing on chairs to reach shelves and moving things around and not much bending over or squatting, so it gave my back a rest. It was one of the few days out of the four months that my back barely hurt and I almost forgot I had an injury.

The next day, the festival came to town and the whole group, including Marq and Paige, went over bright and early to help set up. Now, when Paige told us we were going to spend the day helping set up the festival, none of us realized what would be waiting for us. It literally rolled into town in tractor-trailers and we quickly discovered that the main venue of the festival was a chapiteau (circus tent). The Printemps was a traveling theater festival, just like a traveling circus. The chapiteau would serve as the larger set, while local churches would house the smaller shows.

119

The day began with sledgehammering tent stakes into what felt like solid rock. Since I didn't understand 95% of what was being said, I'm not sure, but looking back now, I realize it must have been a joke between our host and the festival crew—watching me and sixty-year-old Cadence attempt to sledge-hammer tent stakes. We both lasted about ten minutes. In addition to my back pain, my tennis elbow reared its ugly head at the worst possible time, and the fact that the sledgehammer, which must have weighed at least twenty-five pounds, made it torture for my body and a comedy show for everyone watching I'm sure.

Cadence and I quickly traded in our sledgehammers for truck duty thinking we'd have it a little lighter. "Ha" to us. The rest of the day was spent unloading what had to have been fifty-pound boxes off the trucks and pitching the actual tent. By pitching I mean building bleacher seats and laying the performance stage floor. It was like playing Legos with fifty-pound pieces that required two people to carry and strategically snap together. I'm great with tile and crown molding, but a circus tent was way out of my building skill set league, not to mention my physical one. Seriously, the next time you go to a circus or any show in a circus tent for that matter, don't complain about the ticket price. You have no idea.

The WWOOFers weren't the only ones who helped with the production. It wasn't long before half of the town came out to volunteer, as well as all the actors and the crew. Everyone busted their humps that day to make that festival happen. There were no unions, no titles, and no egos. It was a solid team effort and a most refreshing experience—one I would come to realize was the essence of the French spirit.

After a full day of set building, the entire WWOOF pack went back to the house to prepare and serve dinner to everyone. It was by far the most exhausting and physically demanding day of my WWOOFing adventure. But in the end, one of the most rewarding. That day allowed me to fully appreciate every show of the festival that I got to attend, as well as feeling included. I was proud that I had contributed to the festival in such an important way, and it was fun watching shows perform in the tent I had helped put together.

## "YES, CHEF!"
## Just Dessert for Me

If I had to choose one specific WWOOFing task that I enjoyed the most, it would be sous-chefing at Torsac. Since Marq and Paige were responsible for feeding lunch and dinner to the entire cast and crew of the festival, from that point forward it was strictly catering work and each of us WWOOFers were immediately promoted to sous-chef. For the next two weeks, we helped clean and prep the fruit, vegetables, and meat for Paige to cook, as well as serve the meals and act as clean-up detail.

Our mornings consisted of gathering vegetables from the garden, rummaging through the food pantry for all the spices and dry ingredients Paige needed for that day's recipes and sous-chefing the veggies. We would all sit around the table for hours cleaning, peeling, dicing, and chopping potatoes, squash, tomatoes, spinach, and anything else that Paige felt like cooking that day. In addition to us WWOOFers, some of Paige's friends would also come and help us. It was like a little community task force.

Even though I barely understood most of the conversations, those mornings were my favorite part of my Torsac stay. Partially because it reminded me of being home for Thanksgiving when everyone is in the kitchen making the turkey dinner. There were some surprising conversations in English that popped up though, and that is where I first learned that more people spoke English than I thought. It was the most peculiar thing I learned about the culture: many French people can speak English - they simply *choose not to*. Several of the locals I met at Torsac commented to me how excited they were to practice their English with me because they never have the opportunity. It seemed speaking English was taboo, as if it wasn't "proper" to speak it unless it was absolutely necessary. It almost felt like speaking English would be like reading a religious book in someone's basement during the war. They have the ability to practice with each other yet never do in fear of some type of language collaboration labeling.

These "English" conversations were also fun language lessons. I learned that along with grammar, accents also came into play. Multiple French accents were something that had never crossed my mind until it was pointed out to me. Of course - it is the same in all parts of the world; there are multiple accents throughout a country. That helped explain why on the few occasions that I actually knew a word, people were still not understanding me. The pronunciation I learned in one region sounded completely different in the next.

The morning prep was also the calm before the storm. We would prepare lunch and transport it to the Salle de Fete, a few miles away near the chapiteau (most towns in France have a Salle de Fete, our equivalent to a community center). We served lunch, cleaned up, and started all over again for dinner. Sometimes dinner was not served until 10:00 p.m. after the last show. Those were long and exhausting days.

The meal headcount ranged from twenty-five to one hundred, depending on what shows were being performed that day. The smaller meals were at the main house in the dining area. We served the larger crowds at the Salle de Fete. The salle had a stove, large sinks, and a dishwasher, but it wasn't large enough to cook the amount of food we needed to serve. Which meant that Paige would prepare and cook most of the meals at home; then we would pack up the cars and transport everything over. It often felt like we were taking a fully prepared Sunday dinner from New Jersey to my Aunt Shirley's house in Pennsylvania to enjoy "family time."

My least favorite chore was doing the dishes, loading and unloading the dishwasher, and hand-scrubbing the pots and pans. It seemed like for every pot I washed, two more appeared. It was as if my sister was hiding in the pantry and bringing out dirty dishes when I wasn't looking. Thankfully we all took turns and I didn't have to wash every day. There was plenty of sweeping the floors, cleaning the tables, etc., to keep every WWOOFer busy.

The final piece of the day was packing up all the pots and pans, and utensils into the car to take back to the house so we could get up the next morning and start all over again. Since Torsac was the longest I stayed in any spot, I had thought I was going to get a reprieve from the packing and unpacking insanity. Insert the laughter here... Instead of repacking my suitcase, it was a car.

One especially nice thing about catering was working in the kitchen and always being around the food! Marq and Paige were so generous with it for us WWOOFers. We were welcome to help ourselves to *anything*—only the food that was going to be served that day was off-limits. Any leftovers from prior meals were fair game, along with the chocolate bars that Sydney and I would try to hide from each other.

We were the only two WWOOFers addicted to chocolate and it became our little cat-and-mouse game.

While I had spent many afternoons patrolling the streets of France for the next earth-shattering pastry, I accidentally stumbled upon a way to find some of the most delicious desserts in the world without "hopping" while there.

A blog excerpt from _Home Sweet Home_

_One doesn't need to "bakery hop" to have a buffet of dessert heaven. Simply make friends with the best bakers in town. You could experience mind-blowing chocolate tartes, homemade canelés, real chocolate pudding, cassis cake, etc. I didn't hop the bakeries of Torsac, I stayed at one._

It turned out that some of the finest bakers in France were within the communities of Torsac, including my host Paige. Creators of homemade deliciousness like I'd never experienced. I absolutely fell in love with the canelés. Their rich, sweet, buttery bliss was just plain addictive. Having "just one" was not an option. If I could only have one French pastry ever again in my life, it would be canelés of Angoulême. The desserts weren't the only sweetness there either. The people were extraordinarily kind, generous, and as sweet as the goodies they made. If you have a sweet tooth, be sure to make friends there. It is heaven on earth for dessert addicts and what I consider to be the sweet spot of France. They seriously need their own cooking show.

## A SORE THUMB
## What Did You Say?

While Torsac brought long and exhausting WWOOF-ing days, both physically and mentally, it was all worth it. From being able to help myself in the kitchen to the over-all warm and welcoming attitude that exuded from every angle. Everyone loved and appreciated the meals we served them and the comfort they had from being taken care of. "*Mercis*" and smiles constantly flowed. I had a great exper-ience at Torsac and was content I went. I always felt at home there, and by that time, feeling at home was a much-needed comfort. It was over a month into my trip and up until Torsac, I had managed to suppress my anxiety and pretend everything was fine. But the pretending was becoming more exhausting than the WWOOFing work.

I naively hadn't known what to expect around any of my journey, but things weren't exactly what I envisioned. It wasn't that I was having a horrible time, but it was definitely not a walk in the park either. The weather alone had made me miserable; I had frozen practically everywhere I went. I was also challenged physically at every WWOOFing location and my back injury exacerbated the difficulty.

Add that to the exhaustion of moving from one place to another every ten days or so requiring the packing and unpacking of my suitcase, and the overwhelming anxiety of what the next WWOOFing location experience would be like, was all a little much. The fear of a bad experience was quite high as it was all a gamble in the end. In truth, I was constantly on pins and needles and felt out of place like a sore thumb. Not because I was in a foreign country where I couldn't understand the language, but in general with my own life. I didn't know where I belonged or what my future held. I often felt like I was in an episode of the *Twilight Zone*. I once again had to admit to myself that I was scared, lonely, and had no idea what I was doing. My reality - I was in the middle of France and there was no "call mom" option.

Thankfully, the comforts of Torsac in some ways allowed me to ease up on myself a tad. I was able to enjoy some of the moments of the adventure as they presented themselves, like morning prep time, and I began to gradually lose some of the odd, out-of-place feelings. I was still on edge, but I was able to relax a bit and breathe deeper.

Jacqui, a fellow French WWOOFer born and raised in France, played a large role in my overall comfort level. She worked with me almost every night my entire stay, tutoring me in French. She was so kind and I was so eager to learn that I wrote down every phrase she taught me in my journal. Yet I didn't get it. There were times when we were discussing a specific phrase or sentence and I knew exactly what she was saying, yet I still couldn't understand it when she spoke it to me. That was extremely frustrating, especially since I was trying so hard. But I guess that is part of the learning process. If it were easy, everyone would be multilingual.

The most important piece of language I learned was my first curse word. One of the theatre actors, Dominque, spoke English and was never shy to speak it with me. One afternoon as he was leaving to perform, I told him, "Break a leg," and he quickly corrected me with "*Merde*" (meaning shit) and told me that is the French equivalent. That one was easy to remember. He also taught me my favorite phrases of "*C'est cela oui*" (a sarcastic way of brushing someone off; our equivalent of "whatever"). At least, that is how I use it, so I'm hoping I'm right. And the most useful phrase of all, *"C'est pas grave"* (A casual way to say, "No big deal" or "It's all good").

In Memory of Dominque

## A TALENT MYRIAD
# Music to My Ears

I was rarely disappointed with anything in France, but the radio was one of them. I had expected pure French accordion, café-style tunes to be piping out of all the airwaves. Instead, it was like the time I went to New Orleans expecting jazz night and day only to hear nothing but club music. Almost always, the French radio I heard played American music no matter where I was—cafés, the occasional car ride with a host, hotels, etc. I found that so odd especially since it was a country full of music festivals—with French lyrics and French artists.

The music joke on me happened my first afternoon in Torsac, there was a lot of music going on there. Marq and Paige took us all to a music festival hosted by the nearby Steinway piano dealer. The fact that there was a Steinway dealer in the middle of the country was entertainment enough. In Paris sure, but one in the country made it a fun discovery. Even though the showroom was small with only a few display rooms, there was music everywhere you went. The dealer had various stations set up for performers, and in the main showroom section, everyone was welcome to sit and play the demo pianos. Since I barely know chopsticks, I left that to the talented piano players.

The main performance was by a rock singer named Greg Sauzet at the outdoor center stage. And yes, he sang every song in English! I'm a rocker, so I absolutely loved it and was happy to forego French lyrics on this one. My favorite song was about going to live in the sunshine. Which is exactly what I planned to do when I got home—move to California. I bought the CD for €10. Besides wine and macarons, it was the best Euros I spent on the trip.

The next morning I found the stereo in the dining area with a huge stack of CDs. There easily had to have been 200+, and sadly they were mostly either American or British. It was a nice reprieve in some ways from the French language environment because most of the time I didn't understand conversations, but it was also a letdown. However, there was a bright side to the collection. After days of sifting through the piles, I found my favorite French music CD buried in between the Beatles and ZZ Top called *Paris Musette, Living and Manouche*. It's full of the accordion and was the "French" music I had craved since I landed.

The Printemps Chapiteau Theater Festival cured my disappointment of not hearing the traditional French music on the radio. Many of the shows and concerts had the accordion. It was the best live French music I had ever heard. The musicians could have had their own major tour.

Our WWOOF posse spent most of our time either cooking and serving food to the performers or watching them in action. It felt like a two-week Broadway intensive. All WWOOFers were welcome to go to any of the shows that didn't interfere with mealtimes and Marq and Paige always made sure that we had a way to get to them. They would drive us themselves or find us rides with their friends. We lived and breathed the Printemps Chapiteau Theater Festival.

The talent level of all the performers was extraordinary. Some of the performances were more of a show than a concert. They had a variety of genres and were mostly held in a small, beautiful church that sat on the hillside next to fields of grass and wildflowers. It was like I was living in a theatrical postcard.

(Keep in mind that like the movie at Simone's, I did not understand two words of any of the shows the entire time and still loved them. I can only imagine how much more I would have enjoyed them if I had understood what was actually being said.) My favorite show was called the "Frerers Humains." It was like watching live art. It had the piano, guitar, poetry, and, of course, the accordion. It was simply magical.

There was a one-woman show by a lovely girl named Camille. She spoke some English and told me that she had some family living in Oklahoma near Tulsa. I told her it was a small world because I had cousins there too. I wasn't quite sure what her show was about but I enjoyed it nonetheless.

The festival finale was a group musical number that included half of the townspeople. I would not want to be the choreographer for that one. There were at least twenty-five people, maybe more. They had rehearsed and prepared for months. You could tell the festival was important to them and they all gleamed with pride as they performed. It was lovely to watch. My favorite scene was Anne Sée's stage walk.

Throughout the festival, one thing was crystal clear: everyone involved were some of the hardest working people I've ever met. Just as with the pitching of the tent at the beginning, every single person continued to pitch in with whatever needed to be done and it was a big solid of teamwork.

Actress Anne Sée performing

## THE CRUSH OF TORSAC
### Enough Already

I went on this trip with no expectations whatsoever about the men I would meet. I anticipated making new friends and learning about the culture, but certainly no preconceived ideas about men and French romance. Truth be told, I was still processing the effects of divorce and hadn't dated much. For the most part, I had been in relationships most of my adult life and had never spread my adulthood romantic wings. This area of my life since divorce had been worse than high school—full of awkwardness and feeling just plain uncomfortable in dating situations. And my door at home had certainly not been beaten down, that's for sure.

I guess there was a secret part of me though that was hoping to meet the man of my dreams while I was there. I didn't know what he looked like or where I might find him, but that surely I would meet at least one dreamboat. And who knows, perhaps I did and simply overlooked him because I was too busy being an uncomfortable, freaking out train wreck. Sort of like what happened in Torsac.

There were lots of sparks flying, although I wasn't feeling most of them. A local artist hit on me at one of the Printemps shows I attended. (Broken language, but it was clear.) He was renting an apartment from my hosts across the street from the main house. I had seen him around the entire time I was there but hadn't spoken to him. Primarily because he was usually with his girlfriend and small child. When I asked him about his "*petite amie*" (girlfriend), he quickly corrected me and said she was his, "*amie, pas petite amie.*" Ah, the "just friends" theme. The code cracked so quickly. I would find out later this was a standard French tactic. I was not attracted to him in any way, shape, or form, so this was a no-brainer. Next...

Thankfully, not all the men at Torsac were cut from the same cloth. There were two WWOOFers who were rather smitten with me and both of them spoke fluent English. WWOOFer number one, let's call him Patrick, came out of left field for me as he was maybe all of twenty-five. I thought he was crazy and didn't understand why a younger guy would be more interested in me than a young hottie. At one point during my stay there, I had a conversation with a fellow female WWOOFer on the age topic. It turned out that she had had a fling with a guy twenty years older than her a few years prior and she was only twenty-four.

It goes to show how hypocritical we can be about this subject for ourselves. If the roles had been reversed, it wouldn't have been an issue. There have been older men that I have been attracted to. Did I look at myself differently because of this? No. Would I have had a problem being with an older man due to his age if I had been attracted to him? No. So why would I have an issue with the opposite happening to me?

I'll admit, Patrick was extremely good-looking, with a warm and alluring smile and personality. I knew I was being completely hypocritical, but I couldn't help it. It was how I felt. I couldn't begin to bring myself to go there.

WWOOFer Number Two, let's call him Roger. While I'm sure he was still younger than me, he was much closer to my age than Patrick. He too was a sweetheart and a genuinely good person. But for me, there was no attraction there romantically.

Another reason I completely wrote off both WWOOFers was because *I* had a crush on the accordion player from the Printemps festival. It was like a Hollywood love triangle that never happened. He was usually among the group that we catered to every day and I attended all of his shows. He was tall, handsome, and daily workout muscular. He also had a warm smile and was always polite. But what genuinely got me however, was his talent. He played the accordion so beautifully; by his first show I was hooked. Even though he spoke no English and conversations were limited, I had spoken with him a few times throughout the festival but I didn't know his name, and I was too shy to ask.

By the festival's end, I finally got up the courage to go for it. The last evening was a large musical production followed by a potluck dinner. Which meant all of us WWOOFers had the evening free since we were not serving. I spent an extra thirty minutes getting ready. It was one of maybe three times my entire trip that I got dolled up while at a WWOOFing location. I was also a little nervous. I truly had no idea what I was going to say, especially since I couldn't speak French that well. I wasn't going to be able to make that much small talk, and there was the fear of not understanding what he might say to me. The anticipation was quite stressful.

I finally finished getting ready and went to the main house to meet the other WWOOFers to leave for the show. When I asked which part of the show Mr. Accordion would be performing in, I found out he had left! The one man I wanted to hook up with was gone! He and another musician were not going to be in the final production and had left for their next gig. I was crushed. It was a harsh reminder of why I hated dating and the perpetual emotional roller coaster ride it brings. Damn my procrastination and dating fear!

# SAINT-ÉMILION
## Grand Cru

The coolest thing I learned about French wine is that it doesn't matter what region you are in or which grape you are having, they are all delicious. While going to an official wine tasting is fun, in my opinion, you don't need to do so to have a tasting experience in France. You could have a luscious wine tasting anywhere by simply going from one café to the next. For me, the house wine at a local café was better than most of the everyday wines we drink here at home. I didn't have one bad glass of wine at any restaurant, café, or wine bar—not one. In fact, I often liked the less expensive wines much more than the nicer ones. And that is not a budgetary viewpoint; it's all about taste. Even the boxed wine in Torsac was all we drank. You take the refillable inside bag to the market for refills. Then bring them home and put them back into the box dispenser. It's like refilling water bottles. Fast, easy, and inexpensive.

I'm not trying to discourage traditional wine tasting, I did plenty. I'm just saying it's not necessary in order for you to enjoy the wonderful wines of France. Also, shipping is crazy expensive so even when you find one you are in love with, it will cost a small fortune to send it home. You need to plan your suitcase packing around the bottles if you opt to bring them back with you. For me, it wasn't worth the hassle and expense. And of course my already full suitcase.

Saint-Émilion produces some of the most expensive wines in France. It is also one of the most beautiful places I visited. The views as the taxi drove in from the Bordeaux train station were exquisite. I was engulfed with pure awe and actually gasped as we drove through. Lush green fields of grape vines painted both sides of the country road leading up to the small village. The grape leaves were so big and beautiful, it felt like they were welcoming me with open arms and were elated that I had come to visit.

I arrived in the afternoon and decided to go straight to the wine trolley train that went around the outskirts of the town and made a tasting stop. It was a quick trip, but oh so beautiful. The wine however, was not so breathtaking. Honestly, I liked the wines of Saint-Émilion the least of all I tried—*as wine connoisseurs drop their glasses in shock*. The "tastings" were also only a few splashes, far from the full glasses of Reims and tastings that I had quickly grown accustomed to since my arrival. (So says the champagne snob.)

The actual vineyards were surprisingly tiny compared to those I have visited at home. In my mind I envisioned field after field, yet the one I visited is only three hectares. And at the time, it only produced 10,000 bottles per year. They also only sold direct to consumers; their wine was not in restaurants or wine shops. There was a British couple tasting with me and they were as perplexed as I was. We didn't understand how a small vineyard could survive selling privately with such low volume and low prices. The average price was only €25. *Mais c'est cela oui*, apparently it worked.

I rounded out the day with a casual walk around the tiny and quaint village. It was adorable and fun to explore. You can easily walk the cobblestone streets of the entire town rather quickly. (Wardrobe tip: Some of the streets happen to be steep and the slickest I've ever walked on. It is no place for high heels. If you aren't wearing a rubber-soled, flat shoe, you will have to walk around a few blocks to avoid the ridiculously steep ones. It's actually dangerous otherwise.)

Similar to Amboise, I didn't need to be here long to see the sights, but I was grateful to not have to rush to see everything and I could just relax as I walked. I was here two nights so I would have a full day to find lots of nooks and crannies. I stumbled upon the Saint-Émilion wine school and as luck would have it, it was closed for inventory both days I was there. I don't know what one learns at a wine school but if you're looking for one, Saint-Émilion is an option for you.

I had an early dinner at a café and as I was walking to my hotel I noticed a cute little restaurant on the side of the hill behind the main village. I decided I would eat there the next night.

For tasting in Saint-Émilion, unless you are driving and can't live without the tour experience, I recommend a wine bar. You will get to taste multiple labels from various regions, including Bordeaux, and the staff will guide you to the ones that best appeal to you. Even though wine bars don't provide the vineyard setting, the ones I visited throughout France were all small and run by the owners. Because the owners were waiting on me, I got more of a personal wine guide experience and made up for not being at the actual vineyards. They took time to explain different labels and regions and knew the right questions to ask in order to recommend wines that I would most likely enjoy.

Another required tasting in Saint-Émilion is the illustrious Madame Blanchez macaron shop, where the macaron originated back in the 1600s. Perhaps I had become a macaron snob by that point, but the lavender ones in Chantilly couldn't be topped. It didn't stop me from trying several flavors of course, that would just be rude. Then again, after wine tasting in Saint-Émilion, the importance of macaron flavors fades with every glass.

## A THREE-IN-ONE
# My Crashed Dinner

The next evening, after concluding a relaxing snail paced stroll through town, I went to the cute little hill restaurant I had spotted the day before. I had placed my order, and as the waiter left my table, a gentleman came over right behind him, as if there was a revolving door. He talked to me (in French only) for a few minutes and I managed to loosely translate pleasantries. He left only to return with his glass of wine. He asked if he could join me. I was puzzled because he was in jeans and definitely not a waiter. I also had seen him talking to the chef when I first arrived, so I thought he was the owner. But an owner having dinner with a patron?

Once again I was having a one-on-one conversation with someone who spoke zero English. About midway through dinner I established that he was not the owner, he was friends with the owner and that he owned his own restaurant in town. By dinner's end, I had pieced together that he had a teenager and a baby. He was not with the mother of the baby anymore. Ahhh, here we go again… A girl doesn't need to speak the language to read right through those lines. Like Mr. Torsac baby daddy guy, they were never "with" anyone nor do they ever have a *petite amie*. They are always "available."

After picking up the tab, he invited me to go with him to see his restaurant. So I figured, why not add it to the list of my adventures? Since Saint-Émilion was so tiny, it took only ten minutes to walk to his restaurant in the village center.

I didn't know what to expect to find, since I could only understand it was some type of restaurant establishment. I was pleasantly surprised to find it was a nicely decorated restaurant with a large dining room and a beautiful bar. It was their dark night but you could tell it was a hopping place and appeared to be quite successful. During my private tour he explained that he had a house outside of town near Bordeaux but often stayed in the apartment over the restaurant when it was busy. He proceeded to tell me that I could stay in Saint-Émilion and work for him in the restaurant. I could also live upstairs in his apartment. I'm sure I missed several details in the translation, but when a girl is invited to live and work with a guy, she gets it clear enough.

I explained to him that I already had work plans and that I couldn't stay. He pointed out that I could change my plans, I didn't *have to* leave—true, and bonus points for staying in the ring. Eventually he got it, but he didn't give up. After the tour, he offered to drive me to Bordeaux and see the city. As much as I would have loved to have seen Bordeaux at night, I thanked him for dinner and told him I had a scheduled phone call with my sister back in the States and that I needed to get back to my hotel room.

I know… what was I thinking? The man did everything right. He was handsome, established, and a true gentleman. As I write this, I realize that I keep referring to him as "he."

That's because I don't know his name. Now this has no reflection on him whatsoever. He probably told it to me and I didn't understand what he was saying. Even if I had, I was so overwhelmed I probably would have forgotten it anyway. I mean, within a couple of hours, I had a job, an apartment, and a lover offered to me in the middle of France in one of the most prestigious wine villages in the world. Something I had not expected nor was I accustomed to. At that time, it was something too farfetched for me to process and absorb. I wasn't used to men going gaga over me—ever. I went from dates not calling back straight to "move in with me and be my waitress." That time instead of embracing adventure, I ran the other way. Not my bravest moment.

Yes, if I had it to do over again, I would have accepted the Bordeaux tour and spent an extra night in Saint-Émilion —and perhaps accepted the waitressing job…

## PURPLE FEET
## You Had Me at "Vineyard"

The image of Lucy's purple feet stomping the grapes was the first thing that popped into my head when I thought of working a vineyard. I had even asked one of my hosts in our correspondence if this would be possible. He got a good laugh from that and informed me it had not been the case for years! So, no stomping required.

He also told me I would be arriving prior to the main harvest and bottling seasons at both WWOOFing locations I had scheduled. Despite this, I can tell you, without hesitation, that my favorite overall WWOOFing experiences were the vineyards. But not for the obvious reasons you're thinking. It was simply because they were both located in the south of France where it was *hot*! *I was not cold once;* it was heavenly.

Besides eating grapes off of the small wild grapevine patch next to my childhood garden, which I never thought twice about as we let it grow however it wanted, I knew absolutely nothing about growing grapes. So I was excited to get the skinny on vineyards and learn vine maintenance.

I had never thought of a vineyard as a "grape farm." For some reason, "vineyard" sounds more glamorous and sexier, but I quickly grasped that WWOOFing on a vineyard is *hard work*. In reality the only difference between other farming and a vineyard is that you're working with vines instead of vegetable plants or fruit trees. The hours, sweat, muscle aches, and sunburn endured, combined with the overall love and dedication given to each vine, were beyond description. The individual grape is like a needle in a haystack, yet it was never overlooked, ever. It was intriguing how each grape was important. I will never again complain about the price of wine. In my opinion, any bottle under $100 is a *steal.*

# LANGUEDOC-ROUSSILLON BIZANET
## Pruning the Vines

My first WWOOFing vineyard was the Domaine des Esperances in Bizanet, nestled in the heart of the Langued-oc-Roussillon region near Narbonne. It was a family business at the time run by Poppa and Momma Marty, and their three daughters. (*The Martys have since sold and it is under new ownership*) The vineyard was surrounded by a national park with hiking trails that wound throughout the vineyard itself, complete with stunning views of the grape fields and surrounding mountains. I got to enjoy two full weeks in this blissful location, along with my favorite *comedie de language*.

None of the family spoke English and only Poppa Marty spoke a smidge. By smidge, I mean about ten words. And I was the only WWOOFer there, so I was completely on my own with dictionary translation.

Both Poppa and Momma Marty picked me up from the train station. I could tell from the second I saw them that I was going to have a great time and that they were good people. They reminded me of my former in-laws. (This is a huge compliment; I adore my ex-parents.) On the ride home, I did manage to decipher that I was their very first WWOOFer. That was exciting—and scary. I was going to set the WWOOFing precedence. The pressure was on!

My first morning Poppa Marty took me on a tour of the property to show me their house and vegetable garden. We managed to understand enough of each other to get us through. They were remodeling their kitchen and worked in the vineyard by day, and garden/remodeling by night. I couldn't understand how long the remodel had been going on or when they planned to finish, but he was incredibly proud of it.

Most of the conversation those two weeks was comprised of hand gestures and pure charades. My favorite part of the stay was the unconditional fun I had. I laughed more during that stay than I did my entire trip. Every evening at dinner was like a comedy show. First, because I had no idea what anyone was ever saying, and second, Momma Marty was a true entertainer. I didn't understand her words but I sure did get the ideas. She would tell story after story and her over-the-top theatrics were hysterical. She was so dramatic with her expressions and her delivery. I told her she should do public theater.

Working with the Marty family was different from most of the other hosts because they were from Switzerland and therefore, didn't abide by the three-hour afternoon siesta rule. Breakfast was at 7:00 a.m., we began working at 7:30 a.m., took lunch from noon until 1:00 p.m., and ended at 4:00 p.m. with a three-hour gap until dinner which was at 7:00 p.m. The best part, there was no work on the weekend! I loved this schedule; it allowed me to function as if I were home and gave me plenty of downtime in one large chunk to go hiking. Most of the breaks at other WWOOFing locations were always broken up by the afternoon siesta so you never had a large chunk of a day to yourself, except on your full day off.

My initial vineyard labor lesson took Momma Marty only ten minutes (in French with my dictionary.) To my surprise, the actual labor at the vineyard for that time of the year was a simple maintenance routine. Excluding water of course, there were three basic things the vines required: pruning, weeding, and tiebacks. Similar to tomatoes. This also made the translation issue much easier to deal with; Momma Marty's Vanna White-like gestures did the trick.

My daily vineyard uniform consisted of a tank top, shorts, hat, sunblock, and the tie apron. The tiebacks were small wooden C-shaped catch wire clips that served as the vines' clothespins. I wore the apron every day and refilled my ties each morning right after bathing in sunblock. Because most days were sunny and averaged ninety degrees, using sunblock was as common to my day as brushing my teeth. I had never been happier in my life to have this problem after freezing my ass off the entire trip. The heat was perfect for me and I loved every minute of it.

There were only four of us working in the same field my entire stay. Momma Marty, two of her daughters, and me. Poppa Marty was usually working in another part of the vineyard or in the garage. Their third daughter, if I translated it correctly, was off working in Switzerland. Each of us worked independently and had our own section of vines regardless of how many people there were at any given time, so we rarely crossed paths. Since I wasn't working next to anyone (and wouldn't have been able to understand the conversation anyway), most days I listened to my French lessons (*and nope—still wasn't sinking in*), mixed with the occasional Daughtry. Although, there were some days I opted to simply listen to nature. There were windmills on the hill right above the property. So on the days that we had wind, I enjoyed listening to the swish of the mills. At least until I got scared.

On the strong windy days, the vines would blow pretty feverishly and reminded me of the M. Night Shyamalan sci-fi movie, *The Happening*. It scared the bejesus out of me. Pathetically, I couldn't walk the trails behind the house on those days because they wound around the swishing windmills.

Pruning was simply pulling off the baby leaves that had grown on the main vines. They were easy to find and came right off, just like caring for houseplants in your living room.

Weeds were scarce, I would find an occasional weed between the vines, but only a few per row. Absolutely nothing like I had experienced at the other locations; *Amen* for that!

The time-consuming part of my work was tying the vines back. For the particular type of vines I was working with (unfortunately, I didn't take note of the type; at the time, I didn't understand there were different rules for different varieties), they were to not touch the ground. So they had to be gently pulled up and away from the dirt. There was chicken wire behind each row, so I had to carefully weave the long vines through the wire making sure to squeeze all the leaves through the eyes of the wiring as I pulled the vine through. Otherwise, I could break the vine. Once I had the vine through the wire, I secured it to the end with the wooden clip. I went through handfuls of clips daily. It didn't take me long to get the hang of vineyard labor, yet I was slower than the Martys and was always bringing up the rear as I was scared to death of killing a helpless grapevine by accidental pruning.

The fields of vines were endless. They looked like the size of the hayfields I grew up next to where I would drive the hay truck in the summer for hours at a time. To the Martys the lengthy rows probably looked like a small row of corn from someone's tiny vegetable garden. For me, they seemed at least a mile long and grew longer as I gradually made my way down them. By week's end however, when I looked at how far collectively we had made our way through the field, it was quite impressive. And after my prior WWOOFing excursions, this was easy peasy labor. Don't get me wrong, long days in the hot sun were hard work no doubt, but I wasn't sledgehammering tent stakes or lumberjacking tree branches. It ended up being some of the most peaceful work I've ever done.

## THE COOL DOWN
## Thank You, Mr. Sunshine

07/10/2010

Just as life should be, good deeds do not go unrewarded. Working in the sun all day does come with the price of exhaustion, but the Martys always found a way to make the end of the workday enjoyable. Whether we enjoyed refreshing Marty Monacos (lemon seltzer, ice-cold beer, and fruit-flavored simple syrup) or went for a cool swim, every day had rewarding moments. Marty Monacos were some of the most refreshing beverages I've ever had. I remember one day it was so hot we even had them at lunch.

Swimming was another welcomed and invigorating treat, and we had a trifecta: the beach, the lake, and the river. Normally, I don't like the water that much except for the crystal-clear and warm waters of the Caribbean. Primarily because I'm not a great swimmer and I'm afraid of the water. So I was extremely surprised that I enjoyed swimming in the water as much as I did. It also helped that the Mediterranean water was much warmer than the cold Atlantic. The lake was nice too. Because I couldn't understand anything and had no idea where I was once we left the vineyard, I don't know the name of the lake. But it was clean, pretty, and I had a great time there.

The local swimming hole at the river was our main go-to though. We visited it at least seven out of my fourteen days. The water felt so nurturing after a day in the hot sun and it was fun swimming together as a family. I finally understood what my brother and sister were talking about when they would tell me stories of all the fun they had going swimming with our cousins when they were growing up. (My siblings are much older than I am, and our childhoods were vastly different.) My only childhood swimming experiences were in swimming pools, and those were few and far between. Swimming with the Martys was like a glimpse into the childhood I had always wished I had.

Nightly dessert was cool too. As prominent as desserts are in the French Culinary of Congress, they were not always on the menu at WWOOFing locations. If we had dessert ingredients, we made dessert. If not, we didn't. One spot it was always present in, however, was at the Martys. Most days ended with an ice-cream buffet. We polished off quite a few containers during my stay. Every evening after dinner there were always at least three flavors to choose from. It was the cherry topper of my day.

## AND THE AWARD GOES TO
## The Perfect Set for Solitude

Domaine des Esperances won my "Best Bedroom View" award. My room was on the second floor and overlooked the vineyard. A spectacular way to start and end one's day. The spotless bedroom was part of the main storage garage right next to the vines. One side held all the equipment and casks and the other had a small apartment setup, including a tiny, clean-enough-to-eat-off-of-the-floor kitchen and full bath. Because the Martys were in the middle of remodeling their own kitchen, they were temporarily using the apartment kitchen for all their meals. But with the exception of mealtimes, I had the whole place to myself.

For my alone downtime, I mostly hiked and soaked up as much sunshine as I could. There were rarely any other hikers on the trail, so it was always a serene and meditative experience each time I went. I had finally learned to relax about my surroundings and being in a foreign country by that time, but I knew keeping busy with my WWOOFing assignments and playing tourist could only suppress my emotions for so long. The anxiety about what I was going to do with the rest of my life and how I would do it still sneaked in regularly. Hiking and being outside helped relieve that harsh bolt of reality. Eventually, like it or not, I would have to confront them but I decided it wasn't going to be during my vineyard time. That was too much of a priceless experience to ruin with anxiety. So I went back to pretending.

# QUALITY CONTROL
## It's All in the Routine

The Martys had a bit of a routine for certain days of the week, like market Wednesday in Narbonne. Now that was the market I had hoped for! It was a town square market that spread out for blocks, with row after row filled with everything from fresh vegetables to clothes and street-vendor food. You could get lost for hours exploring and still not see everything. Not to mention eating savory dishes prepared in front of you and delicious freshly baked pastries and warm, flaky, buttery, heavenly croissants. Did I mention the delicious cheese tastings at the cheese vendor who has practically any flavor you could possibly want? Narbonne was worth going to for the vendor food alone.

The food and specialties were not the only things the market had to offer. It had its own personality and flair like no other, with beautiful canals along the river adjacent to the parking lot. So you get to enjoy a picturesque view while walking from your parked car to the market. It was the absolute perfect pairing, like popcorn and a movie.

During one of our weekly trips, a vendor was talking to one of the Marty daughters. You could tell they knew each other and that she was a regular customer. I managed to make out part of the conversation. He asked her who I was and when he heard her answer, I translated his response to be something like, "She doesn't speak French and you don't speak English?" We all looked at each other and burst into laughter as he shook his head. There were comedy moments every day during my stay, and you never knew where one might pop up.

In Languedoc-Roussillon, although I missed both the harvest and the bottling season, I did get a peep into the happenings in between them. The prior year's harvests were fermenting in wine casks in the garage and were due to be bottled only a few weeks after I was leaving. During one of our market and supply runs, we dropped off samples from each cask at a sample testing center only a few minutes from the vineyard. I couldn't interpret if the testing was mandatory or simply their own Quality Control. I did understand though that it had to be done prior to bottling.

That small peep into the process made me realize how important my simple little pruning work had been. Come that fall, there would be grape juice fermenting in casks that I, in some small way, had helped produce and would ultimately turn into wine that would be enjoyed by some very lucky customers. How incredibly gratifying. I then understood that this is the true meaning of working on a vineyard and got why winemakers do what they do. It's like golf; you put yourself through agonizing hole after hole, drive after drive, only to hit that one perfect tour-worthy shot that makes you realize why you continue to play the game. I could imagine vineyard owners taking that first sip of wine that they had created. The overwhelming feeling of gratification, relief, and just plain joy, coming to the realization that it was all worth it. They had achieved winemaking. The Martys were such wonderful people. I was honored to be a small part of that overall process and loved my time there.

My last few days at Bizanet were filled with a French-Swiss language combo. Around day ten, a young man arrived to act as a type of apprentice. I never understood the full story, but I think the Martys were family friends. He wasn't a WWOOFer but was doing something similar. He spoke a tiny bit of English, so for the first time, I was able to somewhat communicate with everyone. That was a bonus. The downside: when they would all be in conversation, it was half French, half Swiss. I thought I had been lost before, but I really had no idea what the hell was going on and felt my head might explode. *C'estais un comedie!*

Before I left the two of us took a short day trip to the medieval town of Carcassonne. It was the Martys' way of giving me a little relief on communication and giving me the ability to have a decent conversation in English. It was a pleasant day, strolling by the wall and exploring another nook of French history.

# SAINT-GIRONS
## The Hut

My most astounding WWOOFing escapades were at the
organic vegetable farm about fifteen minutes from the
center of Saint-Girons, deep within the beautiful Midi-Pyr-
enees mountain region in Southwest France. Similar to
Parthenay, Saint-Girons is large enough to have the modern
conveniences of a city (like supermarkets, a general store,
and a weekly farmers' market) yet tiny enough to have that
small-town, country feel. It emanated West Virginia with
its camping ambiance, windy roads, lush forests, and long
hay fields. Not only was the farm the most memorable for

WWOOFing jobs, but it was also the most adventurous, unique, and fun ambiance experience of my journey. I have innumerable bizarre stories and some of my most cherished photos from that week, and I'm extremely grateful Paul accepted my request.

The farm was also the first WWOOFing location I went to where English was spoken 24/7. My hosts, Paul and Marie, were from Europe but spoke English perfectly, and all the other WWOOFers that week were native-English speakers. I could have full, comprehensible conversations with the ten-plus WWOOFers!

Paul was right on time picking me up at the bus stop. On our way home, we stopped at a local supermarket (which looked like an old-fashioned A&P) to pick up a few items, including chamomile tea. He asked if I liked it and quickly added a second bag to the cart when I told him yes. He commented, "I will buy some for the WWOOFing hut." I wasn't sure what he meant by that, but I decided I would figure it out soon enough.

The ride through town was short; within ten minutes we had turned onto a one-lane road leading up a mountain. It quickly became rural, and being mid-July, all the trees were in their full leafy branch glory. As we climbed the winding road, it reminded me of the street I grew up on, right down to the hay barns and the "kiss your ass" turn.

The double tea purchase mystery was quickly solved once we pulled into the driveway. It turned out that the WWOOFers stayed about a half mile down the road from Paul and Marie's main house in a WWOOFer's hut. The hut was an adventure all its own...

My descriptions and thoughts told here are simply telling it the way it was. I am by no means complaining; it's that some things weren't what I had envisioned, that's all. I was treated wonderfully by all and would recommend it to any WWOOFer who is up for some country adventure. Especially for those who don't care about or need conveniences. It truly was a sensational location.

Now, the WWOOFing hut... it had two couches and a kitchen and served as the community building to the WWOOFing campground and had room enough to house two WWOOFers at a time. It was where everyone would hang out during the off-hours, have meals, etc. One bedroom upstairs had a separate entrance. The hut was built on a small hill, so you would have to walk up and around the hill to get to the top bedroom door. There was also a small creek next to the driveway that was opposite the hill. During my stay there were between eight and ten WWOOFers and I was one of the fortunate ones to stay in the hut because I didn't have my own sleeping bag. Most of the other WWOOFers were in tents next door.

To no surprise, the amenities were not quite what I envisioned. Paul had warned me when I first contacted him when he told me it might not be the right place for me, and I had assured him that I would be fine. How bad could one week without hot water be? This was the twenty-first century. It would be like camping. In fact, about a month before I left the States, I received word from Paul that a new WWOOFer had just installed a shower. Camping with a shower—piece of cake.

Well, you know the saying about "assuming." Saint-Girons was the textbook example. I had *assumed* that even the countriest of country living would at least have an outhouse. I *assumed* that having a "shower" meant hot water in some sort of bathroom-type area. Silly me, whatever was I thinking?

The toilette facility was on a slight incline above the WWOOFing hut and consisted of a plastic sitting chair with a giant hole cut out of the seat and a plastic bowl to act as the, shall we say, bedpan. Once you were finished with your "deposit," you would take it to the deposit hole for dumping. There was a water hose to clean the bowl before returning it to the facility. The deposit area would move every few days, as it was not that deep and filled up quickly. There was a privacy barrier, so you could see if it was "occupied" or not from down below. The occupant's legs were visible while occupying the facility, yet everything else was hidden to maintain privacy. I avoided nighttime bathroom visits here at all costs—I dealt.

As for the shower, it was technically indeed a shower. The water ran over your head as long as the hose was turned on—the hose that provided ice-cold water. Now, had it been ninety degrees with eighty percent humidity, this would have been a treat. But it wasn't. Most days in Saint-Girons were like the Indian summer days of Picardy, with the only warmth in the midafternoons. Which meant you could shower in semi-warm weather (unless of course, it rained) during the afternoon siesta with a high probability you would get dirty all over again when you did your evening chores. There were days I didn't even wash my face, much less take a shower.

# HAVING A SHIT DAY
## Dry Days Are Boring

My farming days in Saint-Girons also had their share of the ever-present WWOOFer weeding, along with some downright wacky experiences. And true to weather form, it rained half the week—cold and miserable rain, sometimes buckets.

I helped dig a ditch one afternoon—yes, in cold rain. We didn't have a choice about the ditch. It was to prevent flooding on the side of the main house from the three straight days of downpours. The ditch kept filling as we dug, but, on the positive side, the rain made the soil easy to move. Eventually, the rain stopped and we were able to finish in just a few hours.

I polished that afternoon off by making homemade jam on their outdoor stove. Their main cooking stove was on the outside on the covered porch. I loved it. It was like grilling on the deck only with a full-blown cooktop. And miraculously, the jam actually turned out like jam!

The most poignant WWOOFing experience in every way was my "Shit Day." Manure is one the best fertilizers on earth and has been used by every gardener I know. Whether for flower gardens or a multi-acre farm, it's what you use. And being on an organic farm that used no chemicals whatsoever, it was the main source of soil nourishment. I was lucky enough to have the privilege of helping this cause.

The farm itself was broken into sections. I doubt I saw the entire property, but the "main" garden as we called it, was a short walk from the smaller one nearest the hut. It was rather large and on a hill so it sloped all the way across and had its own smaller gardens at the bottom.

Paul had purchased a large quantity of manure that was going to be used on most of the farm and it was piled at the top of the hill behind the largest section of the main garden. It needed to be relocated via wheelbarrows to the edge of the smaller gardens for distribution, *down the hill—in pouring cold rain*. All the WWOOFers took turns doing the "shit shift," and eventually my turn rolled around.

So you may first think downhill would be a good thing, right? Yeah, no. Shit is heavy. Not to mention that wet grass is like ice. So when you are pushing a heavy wheelbarrow full of shit down a hill, you are actually holding on for dear life as it drags you with it. Nothing says "fun WWOOFing day" like cold, wet, shit-covered feet sliding down a hillside trying not to spill any and making it to the bottom in one piece. Ahhh… the smell of wet manure on a cold wet day. And let's not forget the part about pushing the empty wheelbarrow *back up the slippery hill* for the refills. My glutes had never had such a workout.

Undoubtedly, the Wood Chopping Day was the craziest and scariest task I was asked to do at any WWOOFing location. You of course couldn't have outdoor country chores without chopping wood—*in cold rain*. I was spared the splitting in exchange for stacking. Sounds like a good deal doesn't it? Yeah, no. The wood had to be carried down one side of a hill and stacked at the top on the other. And by hill, I mean a mudslide valley on both sides. Thanks to the rain every other day, the tall, dense trees were full of green leaves that completely canvassed the small valley with shade, maintaining eternal mud trails. Traction was nearly impossible and my feet slid with every step. It was actually harder than the Shit Day. I will never understand how we all escaped without broken bones or mudslide rides down the hill on our wheelbarrow-toned asses.

Out of all of my WWOOFing experiences, I am most grateful for one single thing: I did not see a snake the entire time. I hate snakes. I can't even look at them on TV. They scare me, and they skeeve me, and I hate them. Parts of the main garden that were not planted that season were covered in black plastic to keep the weeds out and protect the soil. The plastic went from edge to edge, next to the bushes surrounding the entire garden. These sections happened to be in the center and there were no walking paths around them. This often required us to walk across the plastic to get to the other sections of the garden that we were working in. Even though no one even mentioned a snake, nor did I ever see one, I knew they were there slithering under the plastic waiting to bite me. Yes, I know, even if they were there, they were underneath the protective shield. So technically, they probably couldn't have gotten to me, but I didn't want to take that chance. Each time I had to cross the plastic, I ran like a marathon sprinter. Oh, it gave me the willies. I would have walked extra miles to avoid that plastic if I could have.

One thing I was least expecting and had never even crossed my mind was the beautiful music I would have the privilege of experiencing at the farm. That was a welcomed surprise! By far the most impressive WWOOFing musician was Dana in Saint-Girons. He played violin with broken strings—an old violin that had seen better days and was apparently left by a fellow WWOOFer. Even with half the strings missing, Dana's music sounded great. An interesting fact about the WWOOFing musicians I met—they shared the same favorite artist, Johnny Cash. Apparently he was the king of the WWOOFers' playlist regardless of which country they were from.

# WHIP IT
## No Electricity Required

In contrast to the amenities of bathroom facilities, the cooking equipment, *by camping standards,* was first class. The kitchen was comprised of a few shelves and a gas cooktop inside the hut. The sink had running cold water, so we were able to heat hot water and cook any dish we wished on the cooktop. The only caveat was that we did not have a refrigerator, nor electric for that matter, so cooking had to be creative and mostly consisted of fresh vegetables and pasta. Because the kitchen was small and there was only a tiny workspace, each of us took turns doing the cooking. A different WWOOFer would volunteer each day. Sometimes lunch and dinner would be split, while other days both meals were cooked by the same person. Luckily everyone got along and there were never any issues with meal prep.

No refrigerator also meant that leftovers were sitting out all night. I remember while living at *Friends*, one of my roommates would eat pizza that was left out all night. The other roommates and I were so grossed out by it. But after this trip I got it. I ate unrefrigerated food on numerous occasions and not just at the farm.

My best-loved WWOOFing chef was Alex, a real chef! He had graduated from a culinary school in Australia and had plans of opening his own restaurant. Like Sarina, he could make anything gourmet quality. He would take a vegetable mixed with rice and butter and POOF—you had a feast. It was fun trying to figure out what concoction would be plated every evening—my cooking imagination to that point had been extremely limited. Yes, all of Alex's dinners were plated. Not only did his food taste five-star, but he also served us like we were in an elegant dining room.

The highlight dish of the week was his zucchini with brie. Zucchini is one of my favorite vegetables, yet I had never tasted it so yummy. He also introduced me to nasturtium in salad, another edible plant I didn't know of. It's slightly bitter with a hint of pepper. I wouldn't eat it on a regular basis, but it was fun to taste it. I would like to say the same for dandelions, but they are just plain bitter and gross. So those will never happen again.

I had one creative creation contribution to the mix that week: chocolate mousse. I found a half bar of chocolate lying around one day and decided to make mousse. I kind of forgot where I was and I didn't consider what a quest it would be until after I had the egg whites in the bowl. It took four of us WWOOFers to get the them whipped—with a fork. There were no cooking tools, not even an old-fashioned eggbeater in the kitchen. We spent at least twenty minutes with those whites, taking turns whipping them up. Being refrigerator-less, I had to chill the mousse in the ice-cold creek water that ran outside the hut. It was the most work I had put into making a dessert since spending an entire Thanksgiving Day making a s'mores pie with my Aunt Anne.

My efforts were not wasted however. We scraped the bowl clean.

## SPA NIGHT
## A Market We Will Go

Among all the crazy and rainy-day chores of the farm, there was also the fun task of helping out at the local farmers' market on Saturday mornings. That week there were four of us WWOOFers for market day. Everyone else had gone to a concert in Spain. I'm not sure of other WWOOFers' ages, but I'm pretty sure that the market crew was the oldest of the whole gang. The younger ones had invited us to go with them but we collectively envisioned a mosh pit of twenty-two-year-olds and quickly, yet politely, declined the invitation to join the concert fun.

For Paul and Marie, market day was the most important WWOOFing task and event of the week; it was where they made their bread and butter and core source of income. This was the epitome of WWOOFing and why it was created in the first place. Helping farmers make a living is a critical aspect of WWOOFing to remember. At the end of the day, a WWOOFer affects the hosts' livelihood and plays a critical part in that process. Whether you're harvesting a cucumber or clearing a path, your contribution is important. And unlike the often harshness of the corporate world, you actually matter to your host and are genuinely needed.

The experience proved to be well worth the 5:00 a.m. wake-up call. I spent the morning helping unload the van and set up all the fruit and vegetables on the table. And bonus, it wasn't raining! The stand that we had was about ten feet long, like any stand at your average farmers' market. Alex cleverly carved shapes for the visual sell and because I couldn't speak French fluently nor understand two words anyone said to me, I didn't wait on the customers. I simply smiled at them and, by 11:00 a.m., was a professional stock girl. It didn't matter, I was having fun and most importantly, I was dry.

As the crowds died down, we each took turns walking around to play market tourist. This one was the same as our typical Saturday farmers' marketplace. Even though it was on the smaller side, it had all the ingredients you needed, including veggies, cheese, and a few food vendors. You could tell everyone knew each other and it was "the place" to go on Saturdays. Sitting directly behind the main street of town, locals could easily walk to the market and then go to the other shops and get all their errands done in one shot. Because of the small size, it wouldn't take long to buy what you came for and be on your way. A convenient layout with about anything you could want for your pantry for an everyday country kitchen. I found the goat cheese tasting and bought the strongest, smelliest one I could find.

Spending time on the other side of the table that day taught me a lot about farmers' markets that many customers, myself included, probably never think about: the hard work of growing the produce was only half the battle.

I made a killer Alfredo sauce with my fresh goat cheese that evening for dinner. Since there were only a few of us, we all cooked a little something to share. The quiet evening also prompted an idea. I decided to have a "spa night" since privacy would be easier to accomplish than normal. I heated water on the cooktop, went upstairs to the bedroom, and took a hot sponge bath. It was the most comfy, cozy evening of my stay. Who would have thought a sponge bath would qualify as a luxurious spa treatment?

## THE TOUR DE FRANCE
### Simply Walk Off the Edge

I have played tug-of-war with myself as to whether I wanted to talk about the Tour de France or not and give more attention to Lance Armstrong. The allegations had started before my trip began and I took up for him all across France, as even the French were talking about him by the time I arrived. But I believed in him at the time, and I naïvely thought there was no way someone beat cancer the way he had and come back a fraudster. No way. So, like it or not, I have to admit to myself that seeing the Tour de France and cheering him on was, in those moments, one of the top highlights of my trip and I have decided to include it. It is also an extremely valuable example of expectation setting, disappointment, and feelings of betrayal. Most importantly, this is my story and I refuse to let someone strip a piece of it away.

When I arrived at the farm the conversation buzz was the Tour de France and that it was coming directly through Moulis, the small village near the farm in Saint-Girons, at the end of the week. Now throughout my life I had only watched the finish line of the race a few times and didn't know that much about the sport. The race had never even crossed my mind when I planned the trip, nor at any time up to that point. But once I found out, I was beside myself with excitement. I was going to watch the Tour de France and Lance Armstrong, a true American hero! I remembered how much my mom liked and admired him. She always talked about his strength, both mentally and physically. She was so impressed with his healing journey. Waiting those few days were the longest ones that entire summer.

I immediately began racking my brain on what to make a sign out of. Being in the middle of the country, I wasn't sure what supplies I would be able to find. I ended up locating a black Magic Marker rather easily at the general store in Saint-Girons on a quick trip into town one afternoon, but what to write on. It wasn't like there was an office section with a poster board waiting to conveniently appear. I was at a loss on this one.

The day before the race, I had set out alone on my day off to go parapunting (paragliding) in Moulis. I had watched parapunters float in the air from the farm for several days and I decided I wanted to be brave and try it. Now mind you, I wasn't exactly sure what that meant other than float-ing high in the sky with a parachute and facing my fear of heights while feet dangle head-on. Nonetheless, off I went.

There were no bikes at the farm, so I walked the couple of miles to Moulis (thankfully, it was not raining!) I had seen the sign for the Ecole de Parapente in the center of the village on the drive home from Saint-Girons and knew where to go. I arrived late morning only to discover they were still closed and I would have to wait four hours for them to open. I didn't have the inclination to walk back to the farm and have to turn around and do it again. So true to my foodie form, I scouted out food and wine to pass the time.

I found the adorable local pizzeria, Pizzeria du Moulin, for lunch. It sat right on a riverbank with outdoor seating, allowing customers to listen to the peaceful sounds of rapids cascading over the smooth river rocks while looking at the beautiful yet towering mountain that I was about to jump off of. Yes, staring at this cloud kissing mountain would require a drink!

Realizing the pizzas were too large for one person, I opted for a salad followed by a chocolate sundae, both accompanied by a *couple* of glasses of red wine. I thought if I was going down, I was taking chocolate and red wine with me. As I was finishing up and just about to leave, the lightbulb went off and I realized a pizza box would be perfect for my Lance sign! I explained to the lovely owners (in my horrible French) what I needed it for, and they graciously gave me one. They were so happy to help me. My excitement was quite transparent and they could tell how much it meant to me. I carried the box with me the rest of the day. I can imagine what people must have thought, "Stupid American, carrying an empty pizza box around."

At the Ecole de Parapente check-in station, I paid my €60 and with huge lumps in my throat, signed my life away.

They took me and the other customers by jeep up a bumpy dirt road to the mountaintop. It was like four-wheeling in the backwoods. Once we were at the top, they put a harness and helmet on us and explained (in English) that we were about to walk off the side of the mountain.

The good news was the parachute was already open and lying on the ground behind me, so I didn't have to worry about it not opening. Everyone went tandem, so my guide stood directly behind me and was connected to all the same paraphernalia, a bit like sky diving. I wish I had a video of my take-off; I was petrified. The ledge that you walk off was just that, the bloody ledge of the mountain. The overall view was fabulous, looking straight out, but I didn't care at that moment. I was frozen. I couldn't move. My guide kept saying, "OK, Melonie. Let's go," over and over. He ended up having to nudge me forward and basically pushed me off.

I didn't understand how the parachute worked, but it felt like the second my feet started moving, it went up and we were flying. Once we were in flight, the harness turned into a seat, and we were sitting for the entire ride. It only took a few seconds for me to calm down and realize what a magnificent experience I was having. The views of the mountains and valleys were gorgeous and I could even see Spain. My guide ascended us so high at one point that we were looking down at the launch site we had just left.

The ride lasted for about twenty minutes, but I could have stayed up there for an hour. The rush far surpassed any roller coaster I've ever ridden, and for sure, parapunting is on my list to do again. Between my jump off of the mountain and the race being the next day, I was so full of positive adrenaline that I remember nothing of the walk home.

Race day was as sunny and beautiful as the day before. Our entire group worked straight through that morning and were taking the afternoon off to watch. We left extra early to make sure we were there on time. Now in my mind, I was envisioning crowds and crowds of people and us having to fight for a front-row spot. But surprisingly there were barely any people there. I thought there would have been a little more excitement and big crowds flocking in. But maybe when you grow up with an event in your backyard every year, it isn't as exciting as we tourists perceive it to be, or perhaps the town was much smaller than I thought, and all the residents *were* there. Either way, it was a small crowd day.

The race itself only lasted about fifteen seconds as the cyclists passed us. They were going so fast; you saw more of the race as it was coming toward you than when it actually passed in front of you. Now call me crazy, but I swear I saw Lance smile as he rode by and read my sign!

At the time, it was one of the proudest days I had ever felt for being an American. There I was, in the middle of the French countryside, cheering on one of the most successful, admired American athletes of our history. And I hadn't planned any of it. It just happened to be. I was so grateful and so full of pride and happiness. It was an exhilarating moment and I felt insanely privileged to have experienced it.

As for the truth that we would later learn to be, I was holding out hope until the very end. I just didn't want to believe it. Sort of like when you are coming to the realization that a certain person doesn't actually come visit once a year in December. The magical heroism gone, flatlined. Usually nothing much shocks me, at least to the core, but I was devastated. I guess I shouldn't be surprised. After all I've witnessed and experienced both in my own life and those around me. The hardest blow for me though wasn't the fact that he actually did it and lied about it, but that my mom had believed in him and was now being made a fool of. He had betrayed my mother.

There is a wonderful book by DeVon Franklin titled *Live Free* that provides a superb lesson on expectations that now helps me understand how to process and work through moments like these. I highly recommend it.

## THE ENCHANTED CITY
### "All Aboard!"

While the French train system is exceptionally travel-er-friendly with its buffets of schedule booklets neatly displayed in turntables by the ticket booths, that didn't always mean it was easy. Determining your schedule and buying the ticket was rather pleasant. I would go up to a ticket window and politely ask using the one phrase I knew well, "Bonjour, je voudrais un billet pour [blank]," and voila, I had bought my train ticket. Now getting on the *correct train*—not so much. Sometimes track assignments were changed right before departure. Even if you've been waiting for fifteen minutes at Track 2, it may switch to Track 10 as you are about to board. And as you may have guessed, Charlie Brown's teacher was making the announcements on the loudspeaker, which meant I had to rely on the boards. And even if I was paying close attention, the boards didn't always change to the new track number. Like the day I left the farm for Toulon.

I was making my way to the French Riviera and had originally planned to couch surf in Aix au Provence for two nights, but my host canceled at the last minute. Luckily I had gotten the email in time to pivot. Toulon was on the way to Antibes, which was going to be my base for my Riviera stint, so I decided to stay there for two days instead. This would be the first time I was all on my own since Saint-Émilion. The ten-day trek was my vacation time, which was all about me and the sun and, ooh la la, the Riviera, baby! I was beyond excited to get there and was at the track, ready to go.

I boarded a car with around eight other people, got comfy, and then we sat. We sat there for at least ten minutes before one of the crew members came by and told us to get off. I couldn't understand what was being said, but I knew what had happened. The track number had been changed. We ended up having to wait for the next train as ours had left the station without us. I didn't beat myself up too badly over this one though, because most of the other passengers were French. It was confusing for all of us.

I spent that entire ride chatting with a lovely older lady sitting across from me. And yes, I use "chatting" lightly as I had packed my dictionary in my suitcase, which was neatly tucked on the luggage rack between other suitcases and would have been too complicated to dig out. So back to the charade game. But I managed to understand that she was visiting her grandchildren and that she was from the north-ern part of France. Heaven only knows if she understood anything I told her and if I truly had her stories correct, but it made the trip go quickly and was quite relaxing.

Toulon was like entering an enchanted city, with my Hampton Inn-like hotel being the beautiful castle. It is on the Mediterranean coast and what I would consider our equivalent of San Diego. It's a naval and fishing port with great weather and beautiful seashore views. I was so excited to have a hot shower and a real toilet that I almost didn't care about sightseeing. So after what will probably maintain the record for the longest shower of my life, I got dressed and headed out to explore. Like every other new town I went to, I couldn't wait to see it.

I did, however, take a practical approach since I was staying for two days and got directions from the front desk to where the nearest laundromat was. Although I could have done my laundry in the creek by the hut in Saint-Girons, I decided to wait until I had a washing machine. And fortunately it was around the corner.

I managed to get my one load into the washer and successfully tackle the detergent vending machine. And yes, it was only one load, as there was no need to separate clothing. After all the muddy, dirty days I'd had since I got off the plane, it all went in together.

I decided to pass the wait by sitting in the circular courtyard across the street. It was a gorgeous, warm day and I was thrilled to be clean, cozy, and taking a moment to just relax and breathe. But as the universe would have its way, it wasn't long before I noticed a younger, attractive man sitting next to me... and he was looking my way. So I said hello in French, and we started a conversation. Sort of. Now by this time you would think that I would have learned *never* to leave my hotel without the dictionary. *Mais no*, I was dictionaryless once more. He spoke little English, but I managed to understand that he was in the Navy and was at port in Toulon for a couple of days. I also got that he was twenty-eight and he thought I was thirty. I could tell he didn't believed me when I told him I was forty. But by this stage I was used to it and knew how to tell someone my age, as I got that question a lot from fellow younger WWOOFers. Perhaps it was fascinating to them that a woman my age was WWOOFing, and I honestly don't think anyone I met there believed me.

We ended up talking for over an hour as I finished my laundry. At one point, I had asked about American movies and if they were subtitled there. *Eclipse* had been released a few weeks earlier, and being a *Twilight* addict, I was dying to go. The answer I interpreted was no, except in larger cities like Paris. He asked me if I wanted him to take me to the theater to show me where it was showing that week. He also wanted to make sure I understood that he wasn't taking me to the movie, only showing me where the theater was. I thought that was odd but figured he didn't have a lot of money and couldn't afford to take me—but was confused why he was interested in talking to me in the first place—perhaps I reminded him of his mother. I wasn't getting it. But because there were so many things happening in my life at that time that made no sense at all, it didn't take me long to shrug off the confusion and roll with it. I had given up hope of making sense of the men situations that came my way and was now able to easily transition from confusion to acceptance quite quickly.

I folded my laundry and we headed back to my hotel to drop it off. I know you're thinking, "finally, some juicy stuff." Yeah, no. He waited downstairs while I put my laundry in my room and grabbed my dictionary. I know. I can hear your sighs of frustration. I had them too. I didn't know what to do. He was handsome and in the Navy. I could certainly envision him in uniform. And you know what suckers we are for a man in uniform… I guess I didn't want to make a complete fool of myself and come on to him in case he wasn't interested. I also knew that when it came down to it, even if I had come on to him, I wouldn't have gone through with it anyway. He was way too young. Who was I kidding? And up until this point, he hadn't given any "signals"—at least none I picked up on. So, I decided to keep going with whatever this crazy thing was and play along. All I knew was that I wasn't going to be the one to make the first move. Good god, how did I ever get married in the first place with all of this dramatic confusion around dating and signals and *ugh*.

We walked the four or five blocks to the local movie theater, and as we had predicted, no subtitles. I would have to wait until I got home to get my *Twilight* Edward fix. As we went back toward my hotel, we decided to get a drink. We ended up having a beer and nonchalantly parting ways. Now during the entire afternoon that we spent together, I never got the feeling he was "into me," and it was clear he was a genuinely nice guy. So if he wasn't into me, why waste so much time? Did he think I was some sort of sugar mama? Was it simply his inexperience and insecurities, or mine, or both of ours? Was this a French hot mess or an innocent way to spend an afternoon? I had no idea. And men say women are complicated. So, the confusion continued.

I spent the remainder of my Toulon tour living the life to which I had grown accustomed—bakery hopping—wine, more pastries, more wine, with some cheese and bread sprinkled in for good measure. And Toulon absolutely met the princess on a budget requirement. I squeezed in one afternoon of good old-fashioned mall shopping. In general, I detest malls, but I was eager to see what a French mall was like. I found some decently priced, well-made lingerie in the mall next to the pedicure salon. Which by the way, was the only pedicure I had in France. Now I'm sure nail salons existed, but I couldn't find one to save my life. I got the feeling nails weren't as important as hair and fashion. And boy, the fashion was at all price points. What appeared to be the everyday, run-of-the-mill undergarments there were lacy, hot and I'm ready for a fun night gorgeous. I bought a few sets—you know, just in case.

I also ventured to a wonderful marché the next day and found a pair of sneakers to replace the ones I had ruined on Shit Day. As I was wandering along the rows of vendors, gazing at the food and spices, I had a fun surprise. I saw the woman from the train! I waved and said hello as she strolled past. She smiled big and nodded her head. I had been in Toulon less than twenty-four hours and I had run into someone I knew. A sense of peace swept over me and I almost felt as if I belonged. I wondered, *is that what it would feel like to live here?*

Later that morning, I was stopped by a German couple in the middle of that same marché asking me for directions in French. I didn't understand what they said, but I knew what they were doing. Being this far into my trip, I could actually say "I don't know" in French decently, but I believe my accent gave me away. They spoke perfect English and told me that I looked like a local. *I was still trying to figure out what that look was exactly.*

## ANTIBES
## Local Living

07/30/2010

I designated Antibes as my Riviera base and did both couch surfing and hotel. I found my couch-surfing host address without issue when I arrived from Toulon and stayed a couple of nights. They were a nice family with a toddler, and the father spoke a tiny bit of English. It was my first surfing experience, and I was grateful to have a positive and stress-free stay. I was up and out fairly early each morning and would return in the evening. The village of Antibes is small enough to allow you to cover many beautiful sites on foot and the train is convenient for quick and painless day trips to the lovely towns and cities nearby. I took full advantage of both.

One priceless piece of information I learned at the farm was that towns and cities have a Tourist Information center, better known as TI. I figured out early on to get a map the second I arrived somewhere. They have free maps that tell you what not to miss and will help you navigate yourself around without too much hassle. This information would have prevented my 45-minute detour in Compiegne. My Antibes surfing host was kind enough to provide directions on how to get there. I quickly got up to speed and more importantly, I had a local map.

The streets of the village are narrow and full of shops and cafés, and the residential areas are intertwined so you can walk for hours and never be bored. I love to look at different home styles and seek out pretty gardens anywhere I go. I also wanted to get a sense of the lifestyle of the average person living there. Shocker, it did not take long for a wine bar to magically appear. Les Sens (sadly no longer) was the favorite I frequented. (And by frequented I mean every afternoon.) Not only did the owner recommend the most delicious wines, but he also had savory pâté and appetizers. It was a meal in itself and one of those places you knew you would enjoy yourself every time you visited.

One afternoon, I was casually sauntering along one of the many tiny streets, imagining what it would be like to live in the heart of the French Riviera, when an older man (in his eighties) opened his door and said hello. Now simply saying "*bonjour*" is a common courtesy and is extremely important in France. For example, when you walk into a shop or café, you greet everyone there with a universal "*bonjour.*" OK—so it was a nice grandfatherly gentleman saying hello. No big deal and certainly no need for alarm.

We started a brief exchange of pleasantries (as best I could), and then he invited me inside. Perhaps it was an innocent invite and I shouldn't have jumped to conclusions, but going inside a stranger's home in any country would scream milk carton. I'm sure he didn't mean any harm, but I politely declined and scurried off down the street. I needed a drink. I headed to the wine bar thinking, *What just happened?*

The Antibes market was just plain wow! It was the epitome of what I had always envisioned a French market would be. I'm sure being in the Riviera might have added to the appeal, but regardless, it was one of my Antibes highlights. I spent an entire afternoon walking through it, exploring all the vendors and the spices et bien sûr, the lavender! If I lived there, I would try cooking with a different spice every day. No wonder they are the best cooks in the world. My goodness.

## GONE FISHING
### The Trail of Paint

The Cote d'Azur tourist board must have understood the significance of standing at the actual site where famous painters once painted because they designed the "Cote d'Azur des Peinters" walking tour throughout the Riviera. In numerous towns throughout the region they erected pedestals at various locations where some of the great artists had created their masterpieces. When you are at the pedestal, you glance down at the painting replica and look up to see the setting right in front of you. It's brilliant for art lovers! They had guided tours in various villages that took you around to each of the pedestal locations and provided history about the artists and the back story of the paintings.

I took the Antibes tour, which included Monet, Boudin, Picasso, Peynet, Dameron, Cross, Meissonier, and Harpignies. Most of the buildings they painted are still there, exactly as they were in the artwork. It was thrilling to stand in the same locations where these artists stood while they had painted. Silly as it seems for this epiphany, it made me realize that paintings aren't just pretty pictures, but they are really a form of antique photos.

The tour also gave me an appreciation for Picasso. I had never been a big fan. I simply don't understand most abstract and modern art. It's the same with poetry and Shakespeare. It's like a foreign language to me and I need things to say what they mean. I don't have the patience to interpret it or figure out the symbolism. However, after Picasso's *Peche de nuit à Antibes* (night fishing in Antibes) was explained to me, I understood and to my surprise, liked it. Because the tour was in French I understood nearly nothing, but with tour guide charades, I got enough to piece together what originally for me looked like abstract shapes into clear pictures. The moon was shining on the fishermen as they fished, while the women watched from the dock. The scene began to come to life for me. I'm sure this is obvious to most of you, but until I had an explanation laid out in concrete terms, I had no idea.

Due to my Impressionism snobbiness, had it not been for that lesson I would have probably not have gone to the Picasso Museum. Thankfully my newfound understanding and appreciation of Picasso's work made visiting it much more interesting and enjoyable. I looked more closely and attempted to find the different puzzle pieces inside the paintings. I admit, I still didn't comprehend the majority of what I was looking at, but the exhibits made a tad more sense to me than they would have prior to the tour, and I had much more respect for the man. I left actually feeling a little guilty for not appreciating him sooner. I hope he forgives me.

## THE SMELL OF GRASSE
## In the Floral Vineyard

As with countless things I discovered while in France that I knew absolutely nothing about prior to going, perfume making was one of them. French perfume was at the top of my to-buy list. As much as I had acquired a taste for wine, and since a Monet was not in my budget, perfume was my treasure chest. So I thought if I was going to buy it and since I was already in France, I should go to a factory and expand my perfume academics.

The village of Grasse is at the heart of French perfume making and was only a forty-minute train ride from Antibes. The walk from the Grasse train station was uphill, with narrow streets that wound back and forth. About halfway up, I stumbled upon a Cote d'Azur des Peinters tour pedestal. It was of Charles Negra and accurately depicted the hills of the town. I decided not to research about a guided tour for that day but opted to stick with my original plan of the perfume factory tour at Fragonard instead. Creating a way to turn a flower into perfume is an art as well in my book.

The soft, flowery scents tickled my nose as I walked up the sidewalk to the entrance of Fragonard. The distinct aroma as I was entering left no doubt it was a perfume factory, but to my surprise, the scents were not overwhelming like the perfume section of a department store. They were subtle, pleasant, and welcoming.

Fragonard was having a "Year of the Mimosa" promotion with posters of the bright yellow flowers hanging throughout the building. The colors of the yellow mimosa beautifully coordinated with the décor and building itself. I'm including this tidbit because up until that point, the only mimosa I knew about was the beverage. I had no idea it was also a tree. I also learned that mimosas grow abundantly in the south of France; there is even a town named Bormes-les-Mimosas.

The tour was in English, so I was able to finally understand a full tour of something. It lasted about an hour and took us through the factory, as well as shared the original history of perfume making. [14]Fragonard was the oldest factory in the town and had opened in 1762. Most of the machines are now modern however and made of stainless steel.

The small bottle assembly line was in full swing that day, so I got to see a worker organizing the bottles as they went into what I will call the "filler machine."

There was also a line of stainless steel vats with what looked like coffee filters in them. They were part of the extraction process. Which quickly explained is when the flowers are put into a container with a solvent and left to evaporate. Each one was named so you could pick your favorite. Mine was Émilie.

The most intriguing fact I learned was about the older version of [15]cold absorption. Before modern-day techniques were developed, the fragrances of the flowers were extracted by laying the individual flowers on top of a flat surface of cold, odorless fat that had been spread onto sheets of glass. The sheets were kept in wooden frames. Workers would keep replacing the flowers until the fat was saturated with the fragrance. Picture that: thousands of individual flower blooms hand-processed that ended up being perfume. It sort of sounds like a floral vineyard, doesn't it?

Fragonard is like Mumm; there is a small museum on-site to walk through after your tour. It was full of vintage perfume bottles, photos, and equipment (including stills). I'm not a still expert, but they looked similar to moonshine stills. And the bottles were ornate and lavish with lots of gold detail. They took perfume packaging serious even back in the day.

I spent more time trying to decide which scent I wanted to buy than I did on the tour. There were so many to choose from. The tour favorite Émilie was my final decision. I had never owned real French perfume before. It was as exciting as shoe shopping.

## ALMOST FAMOUS
## Is Anyone Looking?

Feeling famous is not just for movie stars and royalty. Most of my time in France was spent in small country towns, and apparently foreigners, well… got noticed. Twice, I had the experience of what I perceived to be the feeling of "celebrity." I don't mean paparazzi or autograph sessions, but rather the feeling that everyone was looking at me, knowing I wasn't a local and wondering what in the world I was doing in their town.

I walked practically daily in Parthenay and often, I got the feeling that I was being looked at. It wasn't scary or creepy like the old men at the pool who sit down across from you and stare head-on like you are an exhibit at the zoo. It was more like the fish out of water feeling you have when you're the new girl at school and everyone is watching your every move but, no one will talk to you.

When I arrived in Torsac for my WWOOFing assignment the bus dropped me off in front of the town pub. While I waited for Marq to pick me up, the eyes from the bar lasered their way into me. It was strange yet fun and mysterious. It was interesting to experience, so I happily accepted it and soaked it all in. I wondered if that is what it felt like for well-known people when they go out to dinner or simply walk on the sidewalk headed to their favorite café. Perhaps I will find out for myself one day.

I did a little recon on this subject in Cannes while walking the red carpet. Cannes turned out to be narrowly below Giverny for overwhelming fun and awesomeness. I could visualize the craziness and flashbulbs of festival time as it was still fresh in the sea air and hear the fans shouting at the stars as they got out of their limos, waving to the crowd and making their way to the red-carpeted stairs. I could feel the sense of admiration they had for one another and the gratitude the actors must have knowing they had "made it" to the Cannes Film Festival. It reconfirmed my overwhelming desire to be an actor. Not for the glitz and glam of red carpets (although that was enticing), but for those moments of gratitude and knowing that you are making a positive difference and bringing joy to the lives of others. It validated what I have concluded to be my purpose in life: to help people. Even if it was for those few brief moments during a movie, allowing someone to escape to a place where they can completely forget about their own lives and situations. Giving back the same escape I had used while growing up in the isolated rural hills of West Virginia. To help provide a way out into a world that sometimes seemed as far away and as impossible to reach as the moon. The same reason I wrote this book, in fact. For anyone that isn't able to travel for whatever reason, hoping they can experience France vicariously, and for those considering WWOOFing, an unfiltered glance into possibilities.

*Red-carpet wardrobe note*: There are a lot of stairs for four-inch heels. Choose your shoes wisely and have an arm to hold on to—preferably of the hot actor type.

# IT'S ALL A GAMBLE
## Catching a Thief

I was so excited to go to Monte Carlo. I had only brought one nice, dressy dress and Monte Carlo was the place to wear it! If you follow no other instructions I give in this book, follow this one—*always go to Monte Carlo decked out.* It's the only way to go.

Monte Carlo offered more than glamour and royalty, however. As I walked from the train up the hill to the heart of the tiny city, I was approached by a clean-cut, decently handsome fellow. He asked (in English) if I would like to join him for the day and explore the city together since we were both alone. So again I thought, *Why not?* I had done most of my touring by myself, and I welcomed the English conversation. His name was Henry, and he was Canadian. It was also his first time in Europe.

We spent the day walking through the exciting streets playing tourist, complete with a tour of the Prince's Palace, the Monte Carlo Casino, and the local Ferrari dealer. As we walked the pristine streets, I could feel the wealth in the air. It was as if it was oozing from the pores of the luxurious hotels and exotic cars parked out front. It was a feeling I had never experienced. It wasn't evil or negative but one of prestige, allure, and power. Walking the streets that Princess Grace had once walked, touring her home, and getting a small glimpse into her world before she was sadly taken away from us, it engulfed me in a fairytale-like way. It was one of those moments when I knew I wasn't in Kansas anymore and expecting Cary to stroll by inviting me to lunch.

As pleasant as it was to immerse myself in the treasures of Monte Carlo, and to hang out with Henry who genuinely came across as a very nice fellow, he just wasn't for me. We did exchange e-mails and corresponded briefly for a couple of the weeks that followed. We compared our new adventures and all the sites we had seen since Monte Carlo. He also invited me to tour northern Italy for a week—I politely declined, realizing that not understanding everything someone is saying, might not be so bad after all.

A blog excerpt from *Lights, Camera, Action*!!!

*Walking the red carpet and Ferrari shopping: these are just a few of my favorite things. To get the full effect of a "star," get dolled up and walk around Grace Kelly's home, and try your luck at the casino and car shop. Of course, by "car shop," I mean look at cars that cost more than your current home. Or, if you prefer water, then, by all means, go yacht shopping. Either one will look fantastic parked outside your penthouse. And let's face it, a black Prada goes with anything!*

# GLADIATORS
## The Romans of Arles?

The Saint-Jacques theme unknowingly continued in Arles. On my way to the next WWOOFing location in Vauvert, I got off the train in Arles by mistake. I thought I had to change trains, but it turned out I had gotten off the *direct* train—c'est pas grave. So I had two hours to kill before the next one.

Upon my accidental arrival, it only took a New York minute to find the TI, get my map, and be on my way. The amphitheater immediately stood out on the map and I knew that was the place to be.

I knew nothing about Arles, but the Roman influence was easily recognizable as I passed tall, perfectly built columns and Italian architecture on my way to the amphitheater. I was slightly taken aback because it didn't feel like France. It felt more like I had accidentally taken the train to Italy.

The amphitheater itself was a beautiful, majestic structure. It had a wide set of steps leading to the entrance and was actually an arena and not what I was thinking of for an amphitheater. The circular design was done in double layers of archways all the way around. I've never been to Rome, but it looked similar to pictures of the Coliseum and I expected Cesar to walk past me at any moment.

It was built sometime around the first century B.C. by the Romans, but I would never have guessed. I was fascinated that it was still in excellent condition despite its age, as I didn't see any crumbling or leaning. Even more intriguing - it's still being used today for events such as concerts and bullfighting. Luckily, there wasn't a fight scheduled that day. I've never been and certainly would not have been up for that one.

The structure has seen its share of remodels too. Back in its younger years, it actually served as a fortress. In this regard, it reminded me of Parthenay. There had been an entire community inside its walls [16]that held chapels, towers, and over 200 houses.

Once inside, I realized how large it was. It looked like the size of a small baseball field. Not as big as Yankee Stadium, but [17]it can seat over 20,000 people. The field was dirt, and the stadium had been modernized a tiny bit with railings, I'm assuming for safety requirements. The stone bleachers went all the way around and had four levels. Parts must have been replicated, but it certainly felt and looked original.

As I sat there looking at the field below, it was impossible to imagine all the things that may have transpired within the coliseum-like walls. It was exhilarating to know I was sitting in an arena that once had gladiators galloping around. Gladiators... think about that for a second. I was inside an actual arena where gladiators once performed. Priceless.

The Theatre Antique d'Arles was around the corner from the amphitheater and was just as breathtaking. It was half-moon shaped with the stage in front. It's thought to be almost as old as the amphitheater, but sadly there was only a portion of it that has survived. The seamlessly curved marble orchestra seating remains pristine for its age. I could tell however, in its day, it was a showstopper.

The stage is now a modern platform structure with ramps and guardrails but is wide open and accessible to visitors. As I walked across it, I envisioned a live production, hearing the audience's laughter and seeing the tears rolling down their faces as they watched a Shakespearean play. I wondered what the costumes were like and who the actors were. Was it like our modern version of community theater where the baker sells bread in the morning and by afternoon played Romeo? Did parents bring their children or would it have been strictly "adult time"? My images were almost as fun as the theater itself.

As you walk behind the theater, there are ruins full of mystery and intrigue. Broken pieces of columns and buildings lying on the ground like an archeologist had spread out all the newly found artifacts to take inventory and then left them. Imagine the stories if those pieces could talk. It was a fun two-hour tour, although I could have easily spent an entire day. There were many things I missed, like the Cryptoportiques and the Van Gogh Museum. I am looking forward to returning.

What I didn't realize until I was doing historical research for this book is that Arles is also on one of the routes of the Saint-Jacques pilgrimage. Once again I had walked on the path, but unfortunately at the time, I didn't even know it.

# LANGUEDOC-ROUSSILLON-VAUVERT
## Don't Touch the Grapes

The honor of working on a vineyard continued at Domaine Cabanis, another family-owned and operated business in the Languedoc-Roussillon region, where I was once again a lone WWOOF. *(This too has been sold and no longer with the same owner)* JP (short for Jean Paul) picked me up at the train station and the first thing I noticed was how spotless his car was. JP was a bachelor and I was prepared for the worst. I didn't know what to expect in terms of how clean the house was going to be.

On an exciting note, JP spoke English and was kind enough to speak it my entire stay. Between the English and his entire house being spotless just like the car, the relief was monumental. And it came with the bonus of having my own room and bathroom again. The house was rather spacious and also had an in-law suite downstairs where JP's mother lived. I would later learn that JP had grown children, none of which were working the business with him. I didn't ask about the future of the vineyard after his retirement, nor about the children's mother. I decided those topics were none of my business and had nothing to do with my WWOOFing.

The WWOOFing work was similar to what I did before at the Martys, so basic instruction was all I needed. The big difference was that I was totally alone in the fields. JP worked primarily on the business side and was rarely in the vines, at least for my stay. He would instruct me (in English) on which rows to work in the morning and I would be on my way.

Occasionally, the tractor would make an appearance. I grew up around tractors and even drove them a few times, but I had never seen one like this. It sat up high enough to drive over the vines and all the rows were perfectly aligned to accommodate it. The vineyard was organic, exactly like the Martys, so the tanks were full of natural ingredients instead of pesticides. It was entertaining to watch.

My work started at 7:00 a.m. with lunch at noon. I could work the afternoon how I liked, so once again, I only took a short break for lunch and I would finish by 4:00 p.m. This gave me time in the evening to enjoy myself.

Even though I was again missing both the bottling and harvest seasons, I did have the pleasure of experiencing the table-grape harvest. [18]Table grapes differ from wine grapes mostly in size, texture, and sweetness. Table grapes are usually larger, crunchier, and have thinner skins. They also have smaller seeds and tend to be less sweet. [19]The vines are also maintained differently. Table grape vines are trellised, while wine vines are positioned in a T-shape, which allows the sunlight to reach more of the grapes. I picked twelve crates on my harvest day. Now, I'm sure you're thinking harvesting table grapes is simply picking the grape bunches off the vines… well, think again.

My _Pretty Please_ blog post sums it up best

_When harvesting table grapes, if a bunch is not "pretty," it doesn't go on the truck. (the chickens and field rabbits eat well here; they get all the ugly ones) Also, you **must not touch the grapes**. It makes them shiny, and shiny grapes are not "pretty." When eating table grapes, the correct way is to snip the stem of the portion you want. But **never** "pick" individual grapes from the overall bunch—it's not "pretty."_

And there it is, the proper French table grape etiquette is revealed. Please proceed to your nearest produce aisle to practice, and don't forget the cheese and baguette to complete the adventure. I recommend a bright, crisp rosé to complement your afternoon fiesta snack.

I admit harvesting table grapes probably wasn't as exciting as *the harvest* would have been, but it was harvesting and I will forever milk it as such.

My first official French wine-tasting lesson was at Domaine Cabanis. Now, I am by no means a wine connoisseur and have no formal wine education whatsoever. Prior to this trip, it was only Santa Margarita Pinot Grigio for me. I turned my nose to everything else and pretentiously wasn't expecting to like much of the wine until I got to Burgundy. But one thing the cold weather prompted was my newly found appreciation for red wine. When it's forty-five degrees out and the château you're staying in has no heat, you'll drink whatever is put in front of you. So by day four, I had been hooked. And by the time I reached the vineyards, I happily drank any wine that found itself in my glass and was quite excited for the lesson.

JP brought out his tasting kit and aspired to teach me the art of tasting. The kit had multiple-sized glasses with differently shaped rims. The idea being that each glass produces a different aroma based on the rim. I have to laugh; I had and still have no clue. I couldn't tell the difference between any of them and am probably getting the whole thing wrong. It had nothing to do with the instructor of course. I'm simply much better at drinking the wine than dissecting it. The only thing I look for is if I can see through the glass. If a red is transparent, I know it's not bold enough for me. When people ask what type of red wine I like, my answer is, "steak in a glass."

An interesting thing I learned during my lesson was that wine tastes differently depending on what (and if) you are eating while drinking it. The same bottle of wine will taste slightly different throughout a meal. So if you taste the wine before eating, during your meal, and after, each tasting will vary. It's as if you have chameleon taste buds that morph the wine's flavor.

## HAT COUTURE
## Who Needs Coco

In addition to JP's kindness in speaking English, he also put up with my constant half-French, half-English communication. By that point I had picked up a little bit of the language and made the attempt when I could. Most of the time I only knew a portion of the sentence and spoke what

I knew in French and finished it in English. I could tell he found this odd behavior but entertained it nonetheless. This however, did not work with his mother.

There were times throughout my journey when I chose not to use my dictionary. Sometimes, it was just more fun without it, like with Yvonne, who spoke zero English. Yvonne was charmingly eccentric and bursting with creativity. She was an absolute peach, and I loved spending time with her despite the fact neither of us spoke each other's language. You could tell back in her day she was a pistol. I couldn't understand most of what we talked about and I'm sure she didn't understand much of what I said either. But I had lots of fun trying. I was able to interpret that when she was a young girl on her way to school, she would walk past the prison where her father was being held. I wasn't positive, but I'm pretty sure the back story was that he was imprisoned for being a Communist during the war. As badly as I wanted to know, I was afraid of what the answer might have been and certainly didn't want to bring up any kind of bad memories, so I never asked JP about it.

I also understood that Yvonne had been an artist by trade, and we spent most of our time making fabric flowers and decorating hats. She had bags of fabric and all kinds of craft supplies. She would even make hats out of the leftover plastic mesh from the vineyard—true creativity. Yvonne would have made a fabulous hat designer. I could easily envision her working beside Coco in Paris and designing hats for all the famous writers, actors, and debutants of the twenties. Hat fashion would never have been the same.

## TANGO PLEASE
### Errands to Run

I was on my own for dinner a few nights when JP would go out dancing, and I loved it. A second dose of alone time while WWOOFing. Having the house to myself to vegetate all evening was heavenly. I watched *West Side Story* one night. I had never seen it and was surprised to find it in the DVD collection. *You never know what you will find and when you least expect it.* Like the fact that JP was an avid tango dancer and danced at least once a week. He didn't have a regular partner, so he usually went alone and danced with whoever was there and had an open arm. He took me one night to Nimes. It was fun to experience a French salsa and tango night full of happy people who loved to dance. It was clear JP had been doing it for years; he glided across the dance floor like wine effortlessly flows into a glass.

His dancing wasn't JP's only artistic talent, however. The French, as we know, have made fashion an art form. I found that most of the French, men especially, respect dress codes much more than in the States. While the rural countryside leaned casual, everyone was still impeccably dressed. There were no scrawny sweatpants and holey T-shirts to be found when out and about.

JP was certainly no exception to this and the epitome of ooh-la-la French. Watching him get ready to go out was a show of its own. Complete with ironing perfect creases in his slacks to slicking back his hair while making complete use of the full-length mirror—a true and proper Frenchman. And I say this with love and admiration, as he looked nicer going to the *supermarche* than I sometimes do going out to dinner.

Now after watching tango dancers, having a one-on-one tasting lesson, and overall vineyard experiences, you will probably think I've written this wrong and will scratch your head—but one of the most fascinating things I discovered while at JP's was the public library. I went with JP one day to run a quick errand to the grocery store, and we stopped at the library on the way home so he could return a book. It looked and was set up exactly the same as ours. If everything had been written in English, you could have easily been in my childhood library. You check books out the same way, and the organization is the same: the look, the feel. It wasn't an exciting phone call back home-worthy item, but for me it was like taking another bite out of the French lifestyle. A great example of how we're all similar regardless of our languages and nationalities.

My two-week stay also included a delivery run to one of JP's local accounts: a beautiful hotel in one of the nearby towns. He made most of the deliveries himself and knew all of his customers. Which was no different from most of the small vineyard owners I met along the way. Many of the Martys customers came to the vineyard to buy their cases and were greeted and waited on by Poppa Marty himself.

If you are fortunate enough to live near a wine region and have access to local vineyards, celebrate. You are getting a firsthand experience of what many wine drinkers have to extrapolate from a wine bottle they have purchased in a fluorescent-lit liquor store. There is no backstory to be heard or peaceful ambiance of a vineyard at sunset to complement the wine you are buying while strolling down aisle six. Many buyers, myself included, rely only upon a recommendation from a wine magazine or simply the aesthetics of the label. For me, the label is the window to the wine's soul. It's a wine buyer's guide to the personality and essence of the wine and the vineyard. If the label doesn't grasp my attention, I keep moving.

While going by this approach for everyday purchases works, there is nothing like being at the vineyard in person. This might sound crazy, but whenever I go to a vineyard and hear the owner's story while gazing out at the vines growing out back, the wine tastes different. It's sort of like when you make dinner for yourself and it's OK, you can eat it. But if someone else makes the same thing for you, it tastes so much better. Getting the history firsthand and having a front-row seat creates a personalized experience.

If you are a wine drinker and have never been to a vineyard, put it on your bucket list. It doesn't have to be to an exotic or faraway location like France or New Zealand; it could be as close as a couple of states away. Wherever you choose, just make sure you go. Enjoying a wine tasting while sitting on a patio, overlooking the vines as they smile back at you with gratitude for choosing them—it is a priceless moment. You can't buy that in a duty-free shop.

## DINNER TIME
## The Bellagio Artist

Vauvert was the only WWOOFing location where I went out to eat with my host. This is not a judgment or complaint; the opportunity to eat out either was never present or my hosts didn't have the budget to treat us WWOOFers. So when JP invited me to have dinner with him and a friend in Nimes shortly before I left, I was delighted.

Dinner was at a nice yet casual outdoor restaurant and it was a warm evening, one of those nights you never need a scarf. That southern warm weather, I could not get enough!

Afterwards we went to a fountain show at the Jardin de la Fountain. It was a light show with the water and music. I'm not sure what composer the music was, but it was beautifully done and each note had a water spray perfectly choreographed. It made the Bellagio Hotel in Las Vegas look like a sprinkler in a kiddy pool.

Frustrating lessons around not speaking French did pop up, like the time when I was trying my hardest to speak with someone and they knew I didn't understand what they were saying to me, yet they refused to speak English unless I requested them to do so. I learned I had to literally ask them if they spoke English before they would use it.

We left the fountain and continued on to an art exhibit down the block. Needless to say I had not learned many technical art words, so I asked JP to translate questions for me to the artist. I was curious about his technique. JP told me he would but he didn't think he needed to. He gestured to me to speak directly to the artist. So when I asked the artist in English if he spoke English, he immediately said yes. I had a brief conversation with him about his technique, but that was that. I was annoyed, and even if I had had the budget to buy something, I wouldn't have. That said, for every other moment, I found the French people to be the friendliest, funniest, and all-around greatest people. I absolutely love them.

## BOOTCAMP TO CLARITY
### Life's Curveballs

Often you don't know what's coming until it arrives. Sometimes you just want to throw in the towel, put your tail between your legs, and go home. Then you realize you're not sure where home is exactly, so you might as well put your shoulders back, hold your head high, and charge forward. This is exactly what I felt on my way to Suze, my final WWOOFing location. I was physically tired and mentally drained, and I couldn't bear packing and unpacking anymore from constantly bouncing from one location to the next.

Yet, I had had a wonderful journey through France. I learned a great deal of history, met delightful people, ate and drank some of the world's finest, and bottom line, lived my dream. So if I had lived my dream, why did it feel like I had just gone through some kind of boot camp?

While having all these revelations and epiphanies, as positive as some were, I also had to admit to myself that age was creeping in. I may have looked thirty-something but my body had started to remind me of its true number. I've been active and in decent shape all of my life, but as I gallivanted around France, I began to notice that the endurance was giving me a nudge and saying hello.

The WWOOFing labor had been intense at times, but most of it didn't compare to the thirty-mile bicycle ride I did in Picardy. The other WWOOFers and I went on a supply run to a supermarche one sunny afternoon. I'm being a complete baby here because it was mostly flat riding through the beautiful countryside. But my legs had a different opinion. While I can walk for miles without issue, biking them—not so much. I always found myself lagging behind the other twenty-something WWOOFers on the bike rides, and that one had been a doozy. It was a long afternoon.

After coming to terms with the reality that I wasn't twenty-six anymore, I realized that age is simply a curve ball and decided to knock the shit out of it and continue on with life's adventures. Of course that is easier said than done.

The last of my stops in France were in many ways the most fulfilling. By that time, I had settled in and had a good handle on what it felt like to live there. I gracefully waltzed into new environments and learned to easily adapt to them quickly. I finally felt comfortable. At least as comfortable as one could be on an adventure such as mine, I guess. I could have bailed at any time along the way. But I didn't want to quit or fail. I'd done enough of both to last this lifetime. I decided I had made it this far; I would finish what I had started.

Adele, my WWOOFing host in Suze, was one of the first hosts I had confirmed and was actually another main reason I didn't call it quits. I couldn't wait to meet her. First, she was Australian and spoke English. And at that point of my trip, it was not only vital but also a relief. I had worked my ass off studying since before I landed and learned how to have great conversations with the charade game but I didn't have it in me to go another round of a non-English speaking location. Second, she ran two businesses: a gîte (Our equivalent to a B&B, not to be confused with an AirBnB) and an antique construction material supply business. My original college major was interior design, and I love construction, architecture, etc. Lastly, she simply sounded cool and fun in all of our email exchanges. They always made me laugh and her sense of humor closely resembling mine.

So I bought my final WWOOFing train ticket and off to Suze I went.

# PARDON ME, BUT DO YOU HAVE
# ANY GREY POUPON
## A Pig in the Bakery

My trip required taking a train to Dijon and a bus to Suze. I had a couple of hours to kill waiting on my bus—yes, wine and pastries please! Finding a glass of wine is all but easier than breathing in France, no matter where you go or how small the place you are visiting. If there is a train station or bus depot, it's guaranteed. I spotted a pub the second I got off the train.

I ordered a glass of house wine and pulled out my journal to work on a blog post and catch up on my latest notes. I used moments like these to write, and one's writing is always better with wine. I was not a big journalist but I had kept a decent set of notes all along the way. There were many days when I was just too tired and others when I was having too much fun to bother writing daily. My blog posts were what mattered to me the most and I usually put much more time and thought into those.

I happened to glance down at the table and saw a jar of Dijon mustard. As with the Cognac, until that moment, it had not even occurred to me that I was in the motherland of spicy mustard. I started laughing at myself out loud and as I was looking around to see if anyone had heard me, I saw a cute bakery across the street. Bingo! I could not deviate from the mission now, pastries called.

I purchased a sampling that included a cochon, which was a pig-shaped cake-like pastry with pink fondant. I decided to bring the box as my WWOOFing hello gift. (A small gesture that I learned while in Picardy. It was usually a simple, inexpensive item to offer as a thank-you for hosting. One WWOOFer I met in Picardy had just come from Morocco and brought Olivia fresh figs.)

## SUZE
## Shhhh... Listen

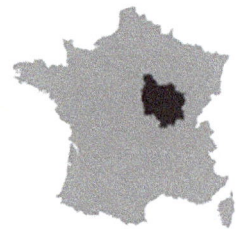

Suze is a tiny community deep in the heart of Burgundy, only an hour west of Beaune, and it was my sixth WWOOF-ing location. It is pure residential countryside with farmland and simple country roads, and there are no restaurants or stores. The store actually comes to you. There was a traveling general store inside a small van that came twice a week. It had a little bit of everything from bread and ice cream treats to toiletries and emergency essentials. It was a mini Piggly Wiggly on wheels.

I digress, Adele picked me up at the bus stop. I instantly noticed her gentle smile and warm demeanor. I knew immediately I was going to like her and felt at ease. It was one of those intuition moments and felt like I had come to visit my sister. It was an unexpected yet welcomed feeling to have found a WWOOFing host that felt like family. It was relieving and allowed an instant calm to swoop over me.

I presented her with the hello gift when we got to the car and apparently, I had done a good job. Her eyes lit up when she saw the cute pastries inside. On our way home we stopped to have tea with some of her friends. We looked at the goody box and mutually agreed to hide the pastries in the car and save them for breakfast the next day. Yes, Adele was my kind of gal. She also had the most adorable accent and I loved hearing her speak French. She lived in England for several years and eventually landed in France. The multiple locations made a beautiful, unique accent.

I anticipated having some type of revelation or epiphanic moments stemming from my adventures but I wasn't expecting them to all come up at the same time, nor that it would happen at the end. The messages and life lessons kept hitting me over the head my entire stay at Suze. It's a wonder I had time to do anything except contemplate.

That first hour with Adele was the most pivotal moment for me on my journey. It was then that I realized I had changed. I was no longer the same girl who had left JFK three months earlier. I could pretty much take on whatever came my way in a calm, go-with-the-flow "I've got this" attitude. It had finally sunk in that I was really there. It wasn't a dream that I was going to wake up from. I was truly living my dream in real life, real time, right there in front of myself. Wow. I had done it. I was in France. It felt so good to finally be in the groove and let my hair down.

This seems a little late in the game, but that was how long it took me to get out of the fog I had been in since that 6:00 p.m. meeting in my office. I believe one reason is because I had a tinge of constant anxiety and was always thinking about things and situations that were coming up: the next WWOOFing location, the next tourist site, the next train, etc. For the most part, I hadn't fully focused on any present moment while it was happening. There had only been a few times that I had truly lived in the moment and been truly comfortable, like Giverny and Arles. I didn't even realize I was fooling myself until I got to Adele's. As I reflect about it now, I am amazed at how I managed to enjoy myself as much as I had to that point.

One realization that I came to was that I wasn't a washed-up has-been, and I still had half my life to live. I reflected on all the things I'd done and experienced and how much I had jam-packed into life thus far. If I managed to continue the trend in the second half of my life, I would end up with quite a full and adventurous package—one that I would be happy to call my own. I simply had to move forward and allow it to happen.

I also learned the importance of listening. I hardly ever remember my dreams but I had one in Suze that is still clear as day in my mind, with a blindingly obvious message that I could not overlook. I dreamt that I was walking down a street and cleaning my ears with an old-fashioned, manual hand mixer. It was bent at a ninety-degree angle so the beaters fit inside my ears and had cotton swabs on the ends. When I told Adele about the dream, she reminded me how important it is to listen. Listen to our dreams, hearts, bodies, and that little voice. Especially when we don't like what we hear, because that is usually when we need to listen the most. A reiteration of the advice Ken had given me about following my heart. It was time to make sure I listened to the listening advice.

After my dream, I was so grateful to have figured out the mystery of why I was smiling and glowing and appearing to be so damn happy when I was let go. It was because I was happy. I realized that listening to that little voice inside you is not always a voice, it can also be a language. Body language speaks extremely loud. It made complete sense now.

There were other life lessons provided to me courtesy of Adele and is why she was the most influential person I met in France. My initial feeling about staying with my sister was absolutely correct. I did not once feel like a stranger volunteering in a foreign country. This also made my WWOOFing tasks that week feel like doing chores to help out at home and not like WWOOFing at all. She inspired me and was an example of the woman I decided I wanted to be and in a nutshell, she gave me hope.

We not only had a sweet tooth and a sense of humor in common, but we also shared other similarities. She too was divorced and making it all on her own. We didn't share every detail of our divorces, but she did tell me that she had not taken alimony either and like me, was in no way being supported by anyone but herself. She got the house in France, which had been their vacation home, and her ex had taken their home in London. So Adele had packed up (just as I had) and re-rooted herself to start over. Well… if she could make it work in a foreign country, I should have no problem on the home field. Hell, I thought if I had gotten myself to France for the summer, the next few years should be a piece of éclair.

In many ways I think we ended up helping each other. I believe I gave her a small sense of inner peace by introducing her to feng shui (or, as she called it, "fung shoey") She had mentioned to me that she had a hard time sleeping, and nothing she did helped. So my first question was, "What's under your bed?" Turned out she had a few boxes of her ex-husband's things stored under there. She had not gotten around to getting rid of them and actually had forgotten about the stuff until I asked. So away those boxes went! She organized her closet and bathroom and slept wonderfully after. I was pleasantly surprised that it worked so well. I am about as much of a feng shui expert as I am a wine connoisseur. I just knew the basics and used what I knew.

I also organized several areas of her house, including her book collections, curio cabinet and linen display. Adele sold antique linens at the gîte as well and I spent one entire day organizing the display in the dining room. The cabinet was an antique and the embodiment of French country living, as was the whole house. I wouldn't call it a "château", but it had the charm of one and was old, but still going strong, unlike the crumbling château in Picardy. There was a beautiful fountain in front that sat in the center of the circular driveway and an original barn which Adele primarily used for storage. She told me I should go stay with people for two weeks and get them organized. It sounded like a good idea in theory, but I didn't feel I cut the mustard for that. How could I organize someone else's life when I had done such a lousy job of my own?

## MORE LAUNDRY
## And Flea Market Finds

My main WWOOFing job for my one week in Suze was to clean the gîte between guests and assist with guest requests during their stay. There was only one turnover that week, so I also did the WWOOFing staples of weeding and cleaning—because, as I knew by then, it wouldn't be WWOOFing without them.

The gîte was a one-bedroom cottage that sat across the driveway from Adele's house. It took Adele and I only a couple of hours to clean and set up for the scheduled guests.

Their reservation did not include meals, but I made a lemon cake to welcome them and picked a small bouquet of flowers for their table. (I asked this time before I touched a flower to ensure I was selecting the "correct" ones.) The guests that week ended up being delightful and they didn't request a thing. It was the easiest WWOOFing task I had.

The weeding was in the backyard of Adele's house, where there were several trees spread out. Adele wanted me to weed around them and clean up a little. She had the appropriate tools, so I was able to create a nicely polished edge around the base of the trees. It quickly transformed the backyard into a tranquil, well-manicured oasis... OK, I might be exaggerating a tad, but it did look much tidier and more polished than when I arrived.

On my day off that week, some of Adele's friends drove me around the local countryside to explore. Just like every other nook and cranny of France I had been to, Burgundy had its own history quietly tucked inside. They took me to Lavoir de Savigny-Les-Beaune, a nineteenth century outdoor wash house (laundry facility). I learned that laundry day was a community event by the river for most rural towns until around the end of WWII, when washing machines began to invade house-holds. Women would gather at the washhouse and do their laundry together. It was a common occurrence like going to the market.

I was impressed by the beautiful surroundings and how well-maintained the lavoir was. Many lavoirs, I was told, were abandoned and decaying remnants of laundry's past. But not this one; it had beautiful flowers along the wall facing the river and sat in the middle of a residential neighborhood full of old, French country homes that are perfectly landscaped with bright flowers, fluffy green bushes, and lush, manicured lawns. It was a true postcard scene. I wondered if it had been that beautiful during wartime. I never thought of laundry as an event before, but being in such a beautiful environment made it borderline glamorous. If I had to do my laundry outside by hand, I would want to do it there.

We stopped at a local flea market on the way home. Talk about market culture; Burgundy was the mecca of flea markets! I learned they had the typical weekend markets, and some of the churches had sales during the weekdays. So if you knew the area, you could hit at least three or four in a week with lots and lots of incredible flea-market-find treasures. You could effortlessly furnish an entire house for under €500 and it would be magazine-worthy. Like the beautiful copper measuring cups I bought for €2 and the gorgeous full-length mirror I found for Adele at a whopping €15, complete with whitewash and all. New items arrived all the time, so there was always a new buffet of quality jewels. It was a bargain hunter's dream.

I had a fabulous time in Suze and would go back in a heartbeat. I only stayed there for a week, but I could have easily stayed the entire summer. A house is not necessarily a home, but Adele's certainly was.

## BATMAN
## Welcome, New Roommates

Whenever I was sharing a bedroom, I was so lucky to have quiet, non-snoring roomies. We got along and had drama-free experiences. I can't say that about Suze, however. I had the finished attic to myself until some uninvited roommates moved in one night. The large bedroom had a walk-in closet and two windows, and it was always quiet at night. By this time, the weather was more like summer. It had been nearly eighty degrees that day and the attic was hot. I decided to open the window next to my bed for some fresh air. I woke up at some point to a swishing noise above my bed. I listened for a couple of minutes until I realized something was flying around my room. I quickly turned on the light to find that I had two bats flying above me. I bolted under the covers and squirmed down to the edge of the bed. I kept the blanket over my head and hair and opened the window as far as it would go, praying they would leave. It only took five minutes for them to fly out, but it felt like an hour. Bats... really? If only it had been Edward...

## THE HITCHHIKER
# Le Touriste Stupide?

I only got stranded once and it was my own fault. I was on my way from Adele's to Rouen for the Impressionism Festival. It was my last long hike across France. I had Rouen, Paris, and sadly, the airport. Only a few days left, and I got myself stranded at the very end.

It was the crack of dawn and Adele had dropped me off at a local bus station to catch the bus to the Dijon train station. I would make the five-to-six-hour journey via train from Dijon to Rouen. I was bursting to begin my festival adventure, so my excitement blurred the early morning wake-up call.

There were two buses per day, one at 6:15 a.m. and one in the late afternoon. If I had taken the afternoon bus I wouldn't have gotten to Rouen until nearly midnight, and I felt that I would be wasting a night's hotel stay, I wanted to get as much bang for my buck as possible.

When the bus arrived, the name of the town listed on its destination board was Beaune, which was in the opposite

241

direction I needed to go… or so I thought. Being used to New Jersey bus schedules with multiple destinations going multiple directions, in my mind, I needed to wait for the Dijon bus. Factor in my sense of direction is one of my weaknesses. There are days I could get lost in my own driveway. Thus, after watching the Beaune bus depart and waiting for forty-five minutes, I found a payphone and called Adele. No surprise, she informed me that bus was the correct one *and* it was also *the only one*. I had just let the bus I needed pass by. She also could not come back to get me because she had commitments for the morning and she had arranged her day around me to get me there so early in the first place. What a mess. By that time it was 7:00 a.m. I was in a tiny little town and had no idea how I was going to get to the train station.

I bought a cup of hot tea at the convenience store next to the bus stop, sat down, and collected my thoughts. I was absolutely furious with myself for being so stupid and not verifying with the bus driver. I could have easily asked, even in my broken French, if the bus would eventually get me to Paris, where I would catch the connection train to Rouen. All I had to do was simply ask one damn question. Sometimes I do the stupidest things and have no idea why I've done them. Those are the moments that I shake my head at myself… and this was clearly one of them.

After fuming for several minutes, I realized I didn't have time to be mad. I had to figure out how to get myself out of this nightmare. I knew the bus wasn't an option as it wasn't going to be there until late afternoon, and I had no one else to call. I asked how to get to Dijon and, well, wouldn't you know it? The answer was Beaune. I didn't know the exact mileage from where I was, but I knew it wasn't too far. This left two options: hitchhike or call a taxi.

I had never hitchhiked in my life and just considering doing it scared the hell out of me. But I knew a taxi would cost a small fortune (at least to me at the time), and I wanted to have as much money as possible for Rouen. It took about ten more minutes of contemplation to decide that I was on an adventure to begin with, might as well suck it up and take the bull by the horns on this one. So off to the curb I went to hitch myself to the train station.

I stood there with my thumb out for probably fifteen minutes. I watched what few cars there were pass right by me as if I wasn't there. There I was, going all in and putting myself out there doing something that I was petrified out of my mind to do and I was being rejected! Talk about ultimate dismissal and complete unworthiness. It was a horrible feeling, and I could not understand why no one stopped. I was decently dressed, had a suitcase, and to me, I projected a nice everyday person. Looking back now, I can only imagine what people thought as they drove past me. I'm sure I screamed, "stupid, stranded tourist." I don't know. All I can tell you is it didn't work and I went back to square one.

I ended up calling a taxi and getting to the Beaune train station by 9:00 a.m. It cost me a quarter of my Rouen budget but taught me lessons I will not forget anytime soon: ask for confirmation, and life is all about choices. Chalk it up to little sleep or simply a stupid moment. Either way another joke on me was in the works. The next train wasn't for several hours and the bus for Dijon would get me there too late for the early train to Paris... which meant late arrival in Rouen after all. So off I went to find pastries.

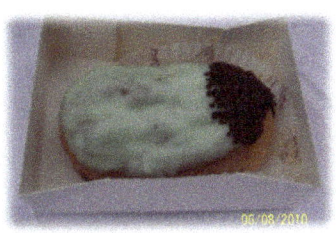

243

# IT'S NOT CHOCOLATE, IT'S NUTELLA
## Just a Taste

I know I said I was going to shy away from my chocolate addiction, but chocolate crepes were a must-have. After all, I was in France for chocolate's sake. I had quickly learned that the French have a love affair with Nutella. I believe one may run the risk of being arrested if making a sweet crepe without it. They even serve it in packets next to the grape jelly in restaurants at breakfast, so one is never lacking one's daily dose.

By the time I had eaten my way through a heavenly Nutella crepe and found the Beaune TI, the town began to open for the day. Restaurant chairs were bustled perfectly along the sidewalk, store doors were set ajar, and the sounds of a new day came to life. As my fifth cup of tea kicked in, I was ready to explore.

Navigating myself across one of the most esteemed wine countries in the world, I did pick up along the way that Beaune is known for its whites and home to my newly found favorite French white-label Maison Louis Jadot. I thought I would walk around and go for a tasting. But to my annoyance, as I scoured the local info, they did not have tours and were not open to the public. (Like Veuve Clicquot, that has now changed.) I did find however, several store-like tasting rooms in the village that allowed patrons to taste a variety of labels, so I went to one of those. The wines were delicious, but it felt like I was doing a tasting at a fluorescent-lit liquor store back home. It totally lacked character and finesse, unlike the ones in Saint-Émilion and Antibes. But I had fun anyway and can say I've tasted in Beaune.

I spent that whole day rehashing in my mind how in the world I ended up where I was and beating myself up over my life choices. How had I gone from having a great life to being alone, barely scraping by financially, and stranded in the middle of France? What the hell had happened to my life and how was I going to change it? My entire life I had always felt like I had disappointed everyone around me and that I was inadequate. And in that moment, I felt utterly alone and helpless. That day in France was one of the lowest points of my journey; it was almost time to go home, and I realized I was in a panic. At the end of the day, I had no one else to depend on, so I needed to step up to the plate. But if I couldn't get myself from Burgundy to Rouen, how would I ever get through the rest of my life? If I didn't know what I was going to do with my life, then what was I going to do with my life?

The anxiety, fear, and disappointment in myself overwhelmed me and it wasn't until I got to Rouen that I calmed down. I told myself to enjoy the rest of my time and that it would work out. Of course I didn't believe myself, but I went with it anyway. I had an Impressionism Festival to get to.

# STOP THAT CART!
## Award Season

I had learned in Antibes that the combination of hotel and couch surfing worked out well at the same location. If one was bad, you weren't stuck there the entire time. So I did the same for Rouen except in reverse. Thank goodness I had because I arrived so late that night a surfer would have probably told me to forget it. I got myself tucked into a quiet room in a low budget but quaint hotel. It was perfect for kicking off my final excursion.

It did not take long to find the Most Intricate Detailed Architecture for International Fast Food Award winner, Mickey D's. Another notable location that was photo-worthy. I didn't eat at this one, I was too busy admiring the details.

And what would a day in Rouen be without macarons? The macaron cart in Rouen put our doughnut trucks to shame. It was beautifully decorated and had every flavor imaginable. Madame Blanchez would be proud. I of course went on to have many pastries while I was there as well, but the cart did win the Best Presentation Award!

# ETERNAL IMPRESSIONS
## A Series for Everyone

Little did I know that my trip to the Musée des Beaux-Arts de Rouen would equal Giverny in surrealism. I had chosen Rouen as my Impressionism Festival destination because the Musée des Beaux-Arts de Rouen was at the heart of the festival in the Haute-Normandie region and only a short train commute from Paris.

The museum's festival exhibit was truly an Impressionism lover's dream. Anyone who had ever been anyone was on display. It was the most Impressionism I had ever seen in one place and was magnificent to experience. But the most breathtaking and exhilarating exhibit was Monet's Cathedral Series. It was one of Monet's most famous subjects of his *Series Paintings*. He painted over twenty different pieces of the cathedral catching various light during all four seasons. Each painting is the same scene, but yet completely different.

Although there were signs plastered everywhere in Rouen that I couldn't read, I didn't know about the Cathedral Series exhibit until I turned the corner and walked into the room entirely dedicated to it. There was a soft, white, backless cushioned bench in the center of the room to sit on and be surrounded 360 degrees by these magnificent paintings. I had seen a couple of the Cathedral Series paintings before at different museums, but never more than one at a time, and certainly not displayed side-by-side. I was star-struck when I first walked in and kept rotating in a circle like a little girl who had just woken up and realized she was in the middle of Santa's toy shop. Fortunately, I had gone at the right time of day and there were no crowds to deal with. I was able to have the entire room to myself for several minutes. Just me and the paintings. I visualized Monet back in his studio, surrounded by his work. I wondered if he had analyzed every detail of a series or simply moved on from one to the next without overthinking it. I could see all the paintings stacked up against the walls and scattered about, with paint brushes on the floor and the studio in complete disarray like a true artist. I think he would have been proud to witness the series so eloquently displayed and organized.

I sat for at least twenty minutes, soaking in every detail from every angle. It felt like I was watching a movie and as the scene unfolded, each season formed in front of me. During the gloomy days, the details were more abstract and faintly sunken. When the sun was shining, the details popped with the light. I could feel the warmth of the sun rays on my face and hear the church bells ring as if I were standing right there in front of it. Then I quickly remembered, I *had* stood right in front of it. It was just outside! The museum itself sits right next to the cathedral, which only added to the surrealism. How incredible. I was looking at paintings that had been painted only yards away. Pure art bliss. The only way to top that experience would be to meet Monet himself… or own one of my own, perchance.

## DARK HISTORY
## Get To the Heart of the Matter

I planned my trip to Rouen solely for the Impressionism Festival, and quite frankly, I had not paid any attention to its historical relevance before going. [Insert Rick Steves' wince] I quickly learned once I arrived that for as much brightness and sunshine as Rouen had, it housed some pretty dark history.

When it comes to bravery and triumph muscles, the town of Rouen is king. It not only is where Joan of Arc was burned at the stake, but it is also where King Richard's heart lies. Literally. His heart is in the cathedral. Back in those days, [20]the division of the body was used to symbolize and mark Richard I's territory. His heart was discovered in July 1838, when a local historian discovered a lead box inscribed, "Here is the heart of Richard, King of England." As my luck would have it, the cathedral was under construction when I was there, so I didn't get to see his boxed heart resting in the church. But I'm sure he could feel my love from outside and appreciated me stopping by to pay my respects.

[21]The cross outside the Church of Saint Joan of Arc sits in the center of Rouen's market square in the exact spot where she was burned alive. The church was built in 1979 and has a modern design of sweeping curves that are intended to evoke the flames that consumed her. It also houses stained-glass windows from another nearby church that were nearly destroyed in WWII. I find this enormously fitting and symbolic. I interpreted the windows to symbolize Joan's legacy shining through each day, reminding the world that while she may have been taken, her convictions were not. She had not been defeated.

Unlike all the other historical locations I visited, I could not imagine those actual events taking place. I didn't want to. I didn't want to think about spreading someone's body parts across a country after they die, nor that dreadful day Joan was killed. Maybe because it was the way in which they both had died and that I simply couldn't bring myself to imagine such horror and pain. I don't know.

I do know that I didn't feel any sense of sadness in Rouen. Yes, it was an intense, somber moment standing there looking at the spot where Joan of Arc had died. Yet, the air wasn't heavy or sorrowful. If anything, it was the opposite. For me, it felt as if it were a place of celebration instead of mourning. The bright and headstrong sunflowers by the church seemed like Joan was smiling at us. As if she was letting us know she is content and full of triumph; she is proud of her conquest and wants us to be too.

# I'M SO ORGANIZED
## Le Havre

I had what I call a "Mel moment" during my Rouen stay. I'm more embarrassed to tell you this than any other story in this book. With all the organizing I did for WWOOFing, an entire summer of logistics coordination, combined with my excitement for the Impressionism Festival, one would think I would verify my research before planning a day trip to a museum. I took the train to Le Havre on the only day of the week that the MuMa was closed. I spent the day walking through town, along the harbor, and took a spectacular photo of the *outside* of the museum. I wish I was making this up.

## RUBBING ELBOWS
## Up Close and Personal With the Arts

One artist I didn't actually meet, but I did rub elbows with—sort of. A co-worker had introduced me before I left to a friend of his, Todd, who lived in Paris, and we got to meet up on one of my Paris stopovers early on. He was kind enough to tour me around his local hangouts and we had stopped for a drink at an outdoor bar. I noticed he kept looking over my shoulder. So when I gave him that "what are you looking at" look, he leaned over and whispered that I was sitting next to Jeff Koons.

*Hmmm*, I thought, *how impressive. I have no idea who 'Jeff' is.* I gave Todd a mini shrug of the shoulder and he discreetly pointed out Jeff's name on the side of the Centre Pompidou and gave me his background. What can I say? Contemporary art is not my thing. But it was fun to learn who he was and helped expand my art horizons and education.

Todd is an artist in his own right. He has a doctorate in Art History from the Université de Paris Panthéon-Sorbonne. He studied Romanesque churches in the northern Champagne region and worked in buildings' archaeology. He specialized in methods and techniques of construction with the goal of obtaining information from the building itself about the culture of the patrons who built it, about the choices they made as well as understanding how it was built, and what the original construction may have looked like. Since many buildings change a lot over the course of several centuries, it's like peeling back layers of an architectural onion. I found this absolutely fascinating.

The beautiful thing about art and artists, you don't have to rub elbows at a table with the artist to get a glimpse of who they are or to appreciate their artwork. You simply need to welcome and absorb the treasures they created. Keeping in mind too, one doesn't need to paint, sculpt, or sing to be an artist. There are hundreds of art forms, such as perfume making, cake decorating, or hairstyling. You could be sitting next to an artist right now.

Then again, I think there is a little artist in everyone.

## SUSTAINABILITY
## First Class Role Models

Sustainability comes naturally to the French, unlike what I am used to experiencing at home. Everyone I interacted with at my WWOOFing locations was not only organic and sustainability conscious, but it was like second nature to them and extremely impressive. I'm talking about all the WWOOFers, hosts, and people I met at various locations.

They believed in conserving whenever possible and taking care of the things that took care of them. There was never any waste, whether with food, resources, or time.

Everything had a purpose and was respected. Even the hosts with the most modern of conveniences utilized them only when necessary. Like dishwashers, only a few of my hosts had them. And even then, they were only used when they were completely full. Or recycling a tub to use in your garden irrigation system.

Every time I hear the word sustainability, I remember washing dishes in Torsac with Sydney. The kitchen had a double sink and while I was washing on the left, he was rinsing on the right. As we were chitchatting away, I realized how he was rinsing the dishes. He barely had the tap running and as he rinsed, he would pour the water from one dish onto the next. It was calmly methodical and somewhat Chopin-ish—each turn of a plate was like a musical note swaying to the flow of the water. A beautiful performance of rinse-water recycling at its finest.

Until that moment, I had considered myself an 8.5 on the water conservation scale. I was raised to always conserve water. The house I grew up in had well water, which meant every summer we were without water at least once. I remember one time the water was off and I had someplace to go and needed to get ready. I had one gallon of water left and somehow managed to take a bath and wash my hair with that one single gallon. I probably used two cups of water for my sponge bath and the rest for my hair, but I did it.

After witnessing Sydney's technique, however, I felt like Eva Gabor. The realization of how spoiled I was and, in general, how many Americans are today, rang out loud and clear. We often take so much for granted. Life has a funny way of teaching us lessons. Who would imagine washing dishes could be so powerful? It opened my eyes to what true sustainability means and I am forever much more conscious of my water usage because of it.

In addition to sustainability, one cohesive theme of my WWOOFing locations, regardless of the modernization level of amenities, was Back to Basics while enjoying life. I've been told that I'm so down-to-earth that my heels drag in the mud, so one of the many things I enjoyed about WWOOFing was discovering what a proud and humble country France is. Their WWOOFing hosts kept things simple while constantly maintaining their "French suaveness." A prime example was the day we had pâté at the farm. We were out in the middle of nowhere eating simple country pâté on a silver platter. It was a priceless French country moment.

## LEFTOVERS' CHARM
## Who Needs Recipes

By the end of the four months, a small cooking miracle transpired: I had learned how to whip up a fresh, healthy dinner for ten with only a zucchini, tomato, and rice. This was almost as big of an accomplishment as getting myself to France in the first place. I never thought I would be able to say, "I can cook" and actually believe it.

For me, leftovers are the most important factor for enjoying French country cooking. It's part of the charm and mystery. They symbolize a gourmet experience embraced at its fullest potential. You never know what wonderful marriages of flavors and textures you will encounter and it's always a delicious surprise. You simply dive into your plate with full confidence that it is going to be a love affair for your taste buds and know that in some small way, it will change your culinary life. Just be conscious to save room for the dessert heaven that awaits your bread-cleaned plate. Otherwise, it's like reading a book and skipping the last chapter.

Dishes made with leftovers were some of my favorites. Now when I say "leftovers," I'm not referring to what you may think. I don't mean heating up last night's dinner and serving chicken for a second time. An example: paprika chicken. Me, I would simply cook the penne, sprinkle some paprika on the chicken, and call it a day; not there. I'm talking about using a leftover as an ingredient to cook a unique creation that can only happen by random accident. You mix today's chicken with yesterday's veggies and rice dish and this giant bowl of deliciousness is created. Everywhere I went, I experienced leftover madness. For those of you who are great cooks, you probably do this all the time. I, however, would only eat the leftover as a leftover—until now.

The only negative of this phenomenon is that the recipes are virtually impossible and always 100% unique. Like the potato and leek soup I made in Saint-Girons. I am proud to say that I joined the elite leftover club by cooking the soup using tomato leftovers from the prior day's lunch. Sadly, it is a dish I will never be able to replicate.

Blog post: *Leftovers' Charm*

*If there was an Olympic sport for cooking with leftovers, all other countries should simply white-flag it, sit down, and enjoy the meal the French cook for them.*

## MY MICHELIN STARS
### Eating My Way Through

My biggest curiosity and goal of experiencing French food was to learn how different it would be compared to our Americanized French versions. Not to mention diving into traditional French dishes that some of us have little exposure to. (I'm a foodie; I wanted to try *everything*.)

I enjoyed the comparison assignments I gave myself. During my off times and transitions from WWOOFing locations, I did a little restaurant tourism mixed with lots of local flair. I patronized all types, from tiny local cafés to fine dining. I didn't go crazy and hit any Michelin-star spots, but some were certainly a step up from a sidewalk café. I usually try to avoid tourist traps when I'm traveling and love to experience the area as if I lived there. For this trip, I was lucky enough to have a few recommendations from friends, as well as my trusty Rick Steves book.

I managed to find more similarities than I anticipated. Like pizza. There were a few days when I was touring around on my own that I got the times wrong and tried to eat lunch during the afternoon siesta when most restaurants were closed. Going against my grain, I ended up eating at ones that cater to tourists because they were always open, and bonus, they were all deliciously good. Their menu wasn't exactly full-blown French, but there was always the American standby of pizza. It was just like our NYC style with thin crust, except for one little detail... the scrumptious, mouth-watering, stinky cheeses. It gave a whole new meaning to *four fromage* pizza.

The biggest surprise for me was the French onion soup. It was exactly like we make it, with the exception of the delicious, real French cheese. I'm not sure what I was expecting on that one, but I thought it would be different.

Now, having access to some of the finest cheeses in the world, one would expect that Roquefort would be fully utilized and blue-cheese dressing would be everywhere in France. Nada. Not a drop. Instead, they love mustard vinaigrette. Apparently, that's as French as the Eiffel Tower. They use it like we use Italian—it goes on everything. I'm not a fan of spicy mustard but eventually acquired a tolerance and I didn't truly like it until I had Momma Marty's. (Recipe in Epilogue)

One sandwich that was on every menu regardless of region, status level, etc., and was always delicious: the Croque Monsieur. It was consistently the winner. (It's also how I now judge French cafés in the US.) It's a grilled ham and cheese topped with extra cheese on the outside. Add some fresh green lettuce with a glass of *vin* and lunch is served.

One food I did not find while I was there was hot dogs. Festivals and cookouts were kicked up a notch with sausage and frites. It seemed to be the barbeque mainstay throughout. I had them at the music festivals and flea markets, as well as making them for the artists' festival while WWOOF-ing in Picardy. The French twist—they're always served with red wine and usually only cost €6 for the entire combo. I'd be at a festival every week if I lived there full-time.

Everyone always asks me what my favorite restaurant was and which spots I would go back to if I returned to France. So I have narrowed down my top four restaurant experiences to share with you. I call them "experiences" because it wasn't just the food that I fell in love with. Each one had its own unique story and adventure that made them my favorites.

I will start with *number four*: Lipp (Paris). It's in Saint-Germain, my favorite section of Paris, and at the time I was researching my trip, the website blasted "In the Mood" by Glenn Miller, my all-time favorite song. I had lunch there on one of the few beautiful, sunny days I experienced in Paris. It was the perfect sidewalk dining day. I hit it at the right time too, midafternoon. (Luckily they are open all day because I had yet again messed up my lunch timing.) There were only two other tables occupied outside, so I had the full attention of the staff, who were dressed to the nines and the epitome of French waiters. Not a hair out of place, their uniforms pressed and crisp without a wrinkle in sight, speaking perfect English with their sophisticated French accent, and treating me like I was the most important person in the world. It was exactly how I pictured a restaurant in Paris to be: exquisite.

I sat between a couple from NY and two Parisian ladies. I chatted (in my broken French) with the Parisian gals and welcomed a conversation in English with the New Yorkers. The funniest part of the story for me was the waiter's comment about my wine order. I ask for a small bottle of Bordeaux, which prompted a response that I roughly translated into, "Oh, you're staying the afternoon." Well once it arrived, I understood. It was one of the largest small bottles I'd ever seen. I had my work cut out for me, but in the end, I managed to polish it off—with the help of a chocolate éclair. *Red wine and chocolate—my theme of life.*

*Number three*: Le Boulingrin (Reims). Todd travels to Reims often and recommended this one. I admit I'm biased because I was so excited to be in Reims, but the service was as good as the food, which was orgasmic. The best salmon my palate has had the pleasure of meeting. And my waiter was so nice and hilarious with his comments and gestures. He could tell I was having a food orgasm. Due to my chocolate addiction, I don't know why I was surprised when I concluded that my absolute overall favorite French dessert wasn't a pastry or even a chocolate soufflé. The winner, hands down, was their cherry chocolate mousse. Top that off with a champagne tasting, and you can say you've lived a full life. And that's exactly what I did. This by far, was the best restaurant meal I had. And it is my taste buds talking, not the champagne. I did most of my champagne tastings afterward.

A blog excerpt from *Cure: Les filles only*:

*Forget an Oscar, this is Nobel-Prize material. I have discovered the cure for cramping! First, you begin with a three-glass champagne tasting at your local cave. Follow immediately with a half carafe of vin blanc. Gradually add two Advil, quiche, and salmon fillet. Then, without hesitation, devour a chocolate cherry mousse (which tastes like a bowl of chocolate-covered cherries). This may be followed with a cup of hot tea, depending on current weather conditions. Continue on with glasses of champagne until symptoms have subsided or you pass out on the sidewalk. \*\*author not responsible for side effects such as theft or public intoxication arrest. Treat responsibly. This treatment may also be used for withdrawals, i.e., modern family or greys.*

*Number Two–* L'Ecurie (Paris). My friend John in NYC, who used to live in Paris, referred this one. L'Ecurie was one of the first restaurants I visited and certainly had the most unique setting. It is in a cave—a *real* cave—in the middle of Paris and located on what looked to be the tiniest street in the city. L'Ecurie is one of those places that, if you don't know about it, you'd never find it.

Once you're inside, you feel like you're in the basement of a castle but in a fun, "oh my gosh, I'm about to eat amazing food" kind of way. I was seated near the door next to the kitchen. My table was the size of a chessboard and I barely had room to sit, much less eat, but it was so interesting I didn't care. I was positioned next to the servers' station where they picked up the food. Many times I heard the waiter saying something which I couldn't understand, but knew it was something to the effect of, "Lady, watch your back!" The food was mouth-watering. I had the prix fixe of pâté, lamb, and chocolate mousse. This could easily be the best lamb ever. L'Ecurie is also only one block from the metro, so even a buzzed American can get home.

And my number one favorite restaurant [drum roll please]: Broc en Bouche Le (Antibes—sadly, is now a different restaurant). I found it by accident as I was strolling along the tiny streets. It's off the main path, and as soon as I saw it, I knew I had to eat there. It had country charm, sophistication, nostalgia, and delicious food written all over it. The interior was decorated like a flea market trade show. There were displays of old coffee grinders, antique irons, and all sorts of things on the walls. The owners (at the time), Fred and Flo, had created a little alcove of "welcome home." It was warm and cozy, and I felt as if I was at a friend's house for dinner—right down to the terry cloth hand towels in the bathroom.

Broc en Bouche Le not only lived up to my expectations, it surpassed them tenfold. I had my first steak in France accompanied with a Rhône Valley red. The best course, however, was the tiramisu dessert. It was a 10.5. With an 11 for presentation and 10 for yumminess. It was served in a "Le Parfait" jar (aka mason jar) topped with a physalis flower. The cream was so rich and thick it was close to butter. It was one of the cutest and richest desserts I've ever had, and I'm not even a huge fan of tiramisu. Another item worth the plane ride.

Along with the Michelin-star-worthy food, I also met some great people there, including an American lady who had recently moved there and her French fiancée. We had a great time closing out Broc en Bouche Le and talking native

English. It was my favorite tourist evening. They invited me to their wedding but it was one week after my departure date, and so I declined.

Undoubtedly the biggest regret of my journey. I was invited to stay, hang out, and go to a French Riviera wedding... What was I thinking?? I believe the most important thing about making bad choices is to recognize them and make better ones moving forward. Easier said than done, but it's a philosophy I instill in myself and strive to maintain. Sometimes I succeed, sometimes I don't. But one thing I try the hardest is being much easier on myself and accepting the person I am. Until I accept myself, how can I expect anyone else to?

## LIVING THE DREAM TOUR
## Freedom

Of all the lessons I have learned since that 6:00 p.m. meeting, embracing the journey is the most important to me. While overall I hadn't permitted myself to truly relax and enjoy the ride, I'm so happy and proud of myself for doing so during my last night in France. I spent that night in Paris. I found a great deal at a hotel in Saint Germain and had dinner with Todd. The perfect ending to my "living the dream tour."

Thrilled to be spending my last night in the Saint Germain section, I buried the panic of "what in the hell I was going to do with the rest of my life" once again, and I was OK with that. I had no idea, not an inkling of a plan, as to what I would do next. I only knew I wanted to get home, visit my family, and let everything settle in.

So my trip ended as it began. I was like a sheer ruffled curtain blowing in the wind, living out of a suitcase with no solid plan in tow. I had complete freedom.

# EPILOGUE

My dream trip to France was more than a trip. It was an accomplishment. For the first time in my life, I had a clear vision of something I wanted to do. I visualized the plan to accomplish it, had the guts to execute it, and, most importantly, succeeded in doing it. For me, this was miraculous.

Looking back, I realize that it wasn't a specific WWOOFing task or WWOOFing location that stands out the most from my WWOOFing adventure. It was the satisfaction of meeting new people and being appreciated by the hosts. Gratitude goes such a long way with me. It's the biggest reward I could receive for doing good things and makes me want to do more. Knowing that I had truly helped them and I had given back as much as they had given me. Most of my hosts were so appreciative and never shy to thank me. Some were so happy with my weeding, you would have thought I had built them a new patio.

The gratitude made all the aches, pains, blood, sweat, and tears worthwhile. But isn't that true with any relationship, though? The more you feel appreciated, the happier you are. It's not rocket science, yet how easily we often overlook it. Who knows how many relationships could be salvaged with simply a "thank you." And, better yet, how many evolve from those two little words? No amount of money or gifts can replace that.

By volunteering to be a WWOOFer, you are committing to a relationship of helping the hosts make their dreams and aspirations possible while learning to shape your own: an irreplaceable experience and exchange. No matter what your age or circumstance, I highly recommend WWOOFing to anyone willing and able.

A few helpful WWOOFing topics to share with anyone considering signing up.

**Language Barrier**: If the inability to speak a language is the only thing holding you back from WWOOFing or even a silly stereotype, update your passport and be on your way. Life is too short, embrace the challenges and tackle them head-on. You're missing out on great food, wine, and overall life experiences. And as I've learned, communication comes in many forms besides speaking a common language. I think the bottom line is if you want to "talk" to someone, you'll figure it out. Have patience with yourself and others. Being kind is the easiest way. When communicating with potential hosts, if you do not speak the native language of the country you are applying to, be sure to ask if they are OK with that and if they speak any English. If so, are they willing to speak English to you most of the time? If not, are they comfortable that you won't understand them and vice versa?

**Type of Work**: The type of WWOOFing volunteer work you do varies depending on the location, business, etc. Selecting your WWOOFing locations and hosts is sort of like creating a college class schedule; there are many areas that you can major in. For example, if you want to learn about specific types of organic farming techniques, you would select farms that specialize in organic practices. Or if you want to learn the art of winemaking, you select vine-yards. It's all up to you. Also, keep weather in mind and choose locations that fit you.

For skills, it's imperative to know your physical labor capabilities and limitations. You may not be the right fit for some locations, so you want to ensure that you will, in fact, be able to help them and won't require other WWOOFers to take up your slack.

**Applications**: The greatest tip for applying at WWOOF is to know and be clear about the restrictions—there are none, truly. Honesty is the best policy here. There is no age limitation, as most hosts welcome people of all ages and skill levels. Whether you speak their native language or can only speak English, some hosts are comfortable with either if you communicate language barriers beforehand. The worst thing for both of you is to get yourself into a situation where you are unable to perform the tasks they assign, and expectations are not met.

It's also extremely important to remember most WWOOF-ing hosts are running a business, and you must market yourself as if you were applying for any other job, thus why I describe this as an application-submission process. Their farm, vine-yard, etc., is their livelihood—and just because you are volunteering doesn't mean they will accept everyone who writes to them. Highlighting your relevant skills and knowledge so that your application stands out and hosts can notice why you may be an asset is critical. If you have certain farming skills or knowledge for their particular type of business, highlight that and explain why you would be helpful. Some of these locations receive several requests a day.

You should also disclose your age. Even though a large number of WWOOFers I met were young college kids, many hosts are used to having WWOOFers of all age ranges. So don't be intimidated by your "number" or let it dictate where you apply to. There are many locations that welcome older, seasoned WWOOFers with life experience like myself, as well as couples and families with young children.

Below is an excerpt from my application e-mail that I used for all of my applications. Note it's in English.

Bonjour! I am a new WWOOF member and would love to come and work with you. I was recently laid off from my job of three years and have decided to take some time for myself to explore France. I have never been there, but have always wanted to go. I am currently taking a French class and am practicing with my French-speaking friends. I'm very excited to learn the language and experience the culture!

I am forty years old, divorced, neat, organized, and a nonsmoker. I am handy around the house, am a seamstress, baker, and hard worker. I've attached photos of various home projects I have done. I have no preferences or special requests as to how I could help you. I'm open to what you need. I am available May 30 - June 12, 2010.

**Packing and Visas**: There wasn't a huge social media outlet or numerous online communities at the time for me to research, and, even though I had done my homework, I still wasn't exactly sure what WWOOFing was. I certainly had no idea what to pack or what I would need. Here is some "do as I say, not as I did advice."

I ultimately looked at the normal temperatures and determined I would pack for a summer in the northeast. I included a few dressy outfits, casual and work clothes. For the work clothes, I took T-shirts, tanks, and cargo pants. I did bring a couple of summer sweaters and a cape, but those were nice ones, not for work. I also didn't think about the fact that many times I would have to schlep my suitcase up and down stairs. I checked in at JFK with a fifty-nine-and-a-half-pound suitcase. I could barely maneuver it. I was trying to be prepared, and my preparedness ended up being my enemy. Not only did I not need most of what I brought, but I also did not pack for fall/winter. So the warm clothes I did bring weren't warm enough and certainly not WWOOFing-worthy. I ruined several of my favorite clothes. Not to mention that, after injuring my back, I physically couldn't handle a heavy bag. Olivia has a tiny collection of clothing left by WWOOFers for WWOOFers so I had even donated some items back in Picardy I felt I was not going to need in an attempt to make the suitcase a little lighter. That almost worked…until I got to Amboise. I ended up shipping three boxes of clothes home along the way at various stops, selecting the heaviest and nicest quality items. These shipping and suitcase escapades also cut into my budget and were a totally unnecessary and ridiculous expense. It was a packing experience that won't be forgotten and has forever changed my packing methods. Regardless of where you are going, always pack a piece of fleece, be prepared for rain, and make sure you can maneuver your own bag.

Bottom line advice—pack as little as possible and take clothes you can easily hand wash and hang dry. Pack for one week and keep recycling. You're not doing a fashion show; no one will care if you wear something three days in a row. People probably won't even notice or will be doing the same thing themselves. One item you cannot pack too many of, however, is socks. Bring plenty of both everyday socks and warm, wool ones for cold nights. And I strongly urge you to use a large backpack, never a suitcase. It's easier and will force you to trim the luggage fat.

Most of the WWOOFing work is outdoors, so bring layers because even during the summer, mornings can be cold, depending on where you are. Assume that you will get dirty within five minutes of getting dressed, so never expect to be shiny and clean, and never wear a "favorite" item that you don't want to get ruined. Also, be prepared to work in the rain and assume it will be cold rain. You will most likely be able to launder your clothes wherever you are, even if it's simply washing them in the sink, but know, in general, that most of your clothes will be dirty at all times.

For shoes, bring comfortable work boots, sneakers, and flip-flops. I suggest bringing old shoes that you can throw away when you leave because there may be some grimy jobs on your list, and you might not want them back.

Some essential items I would not leave without: Individual laundry packets, sunblock, shampoo, soap, Band-Aids, tooth-paste, bath towel, a box of travel-friendly snack bars, and again, plenty of extra socks. For your hair, get a style that requires zero maintenance. Even if you bring a hair dryer, assume there will be no place to use it. I learned that plain and simple is just that: really simple and delightfully plain. I blow-dried my hair three times in four months. *In a nutshell, prepare for cold weather camping and you'll be all set.*

Visa requirements change; do your homework and verify three times you have the correct information.

**Animals, Cleanliness, and Safety**: Animals are a big part of life in France, especially the dogs. Most of my hosts had at least one dog and one cat. All were snuggle friendly and very lovable. The one dog in Torsac was one of the biggest dogs I've ever seen. I'm not as familiar with dog breeds as I am with cats, so I have no idea what kind he was. I know he was huge, and his heart was even bigger.

Dogs in the cafés and restaurants were everywhere and a welcomed piece of scenery from ordinary French life.

The country was clean and shiny for the most part. There was graffiti and some trash here and there, like any city would have, but in general, it was clean. Especially the metro, so much cleaner and brighter than New York City.

Safety was also not an issue for me. I always felt safe, especially when I was WWOOFing and with my hosts. Most of my hosts treated me like I was family when it came to being safe, secure, and taken care of. When I was on my own, between WWOOFing stops and playing tourist, I acted no differently than I would anywhere else. As with any location, whether it's one of the world's largest cities or the smallest of country towns, you have to use common sense and be aware of your surroundings. I never felt threatened or in danger.

If you're going to WWOOF in France, or anywhere that has vineyards for that matter, you must WWOOF at least one vineyard. And even if you end up having a miserable time, the wine alone will probably more than make up for it. By far, the 2008 Syrah from <u>Domaine de Esperances</u> is the best bold red wine I have ever had the privilege of tasting. My amateur description was, "An elegant, full, velvet wine that is worth the plane ride." And for a hot summer's day, Domaine Cabanis' rosé is "porch-swinging" delicious. It's as light and delicate as wispy clouds in the late afternoon; you can slightly feel a soft summer breeze gliding across your face as you drink it. (I wonder if sommeliers have ever used "worth the plane ride" or "porch-swinging" as descriptives.)

I'm sure any region you choose would be fabulous and offer a true French vineyard experience. I'm partial to the Languedoc-Roussillon region for the temperatures, beaches, markets, and, above all, the people. They are fun, happy, loving-life folks.

# RECIPES

## Momma Marty's Vinaigrette

- 1 1/4 C apple cider vinegar
- 1 2/3 C olive oil
- 1 T mustard
- 1 t salt
- 1 t sugar
- 1 T soy sauce
- 1 T Worcestershire sauce
- Fresh herbs of choice to taste

## Paige's Chocolate Gâteau

- 1 Bar melted chocolate
- 2/3 C butter
- 7/8 C sugar
- 4 eggs
- 1 2/3 C flour
- 1 t baking soda

Mix butter and sugar for 5 min, then add one egg at a time. Blend in melted chocolate, then add flour and soda. Bake at 350 for 30-45 mins depending upon pan size/shape.

# ACKNOWLEDGMENTS

(in no particular order)

An eternal thank-you to my birthday twin and true friend, Deidré, for countless re-reads and endless support. You probably have this thing memorized.

To my NOHO writing group for your feedback, patience, and guidance: Angela, Charles, Eric, Everett, Greg, Lauren, Maddie, Matt, Mercedes, Suzy, Trina, and Yvette. Without you, this book would not be what it is and would not have even gotten started. You are all truly remarkable talents *with wings*.

To all of my volunteers (and family members who had no choice) who participated in my survey project several years ago and to my test readers, your feedback and ideas were irreplaceable.

To Amanda Loveland for helping me recognize my book dream and build the courage to go after it (even though it took a little longer than originally planned.)

To Jon for planting the French seed and giving me the encouragement to watch it grow. I would not have thought outside the box without you.

To my roomies at *Friends*, for putting up with me and supporting me throughout my stay. You were family to me when I needed it most. CarolAnn, I will never forget the birthday party and I still feel horrible about the cookie jar.

To Ken for convincing me I wasn't crazy.

To my WWOOFing hosts and all the WWOOFers I met on my journey, you molded the experience that changed my life.

To my D.C. and friend, Dr. Shelley Bosten, who helped me gain strength and get through the past few years.

And finally, to the readers – thank you!

# ABOUT THE AUTHOR

Mel Reyna Scott was a first time WWOOFer at age 40, when she became a volunteer for World Wide Opportunities on Organic Farms and took off to the City of Love. Her service comprised of various assignments, including a vegetable farm and vineyards in the South of France.

Her previous journeys have taken her from the coffee plantations of Costa Rica to the temples and markets of India, and now to the land of Champagne and Dijon mustard. When she's not exploring the world, Mel Reyna is a freelance contractor and producer living in Los Angeles with her two fur children and always has her passport a ready.

@melreynascott
https://books2read.com/MelReynaScott

Photo Credit: William Kidston Photography -
Rest in peace my friend

# FOOTNOTES

1. http://en.wikipedia.org/wiki/Ch%C3%A2teau_de_Chantilly
2. http://en.wikipedia.org/wiki/Forest_of_Compi%C3%A8gne
3. http://en.wikipedia.org/wiki/Forest_of_Compi%C3%A8gne
4. http://picardietourisme.com/en/nos-idees-de-weekend/nos-suggestions/the-armistice-glade-09f.aspx
5. http://picardietourisme.com/en/nos-idees-de-weekend/nos-suggestions/the-armistice-glade-09f.aspx
6. http://en.wikipedia.org/wiki/Ferdinand_Foch
7. http://en.wikipedia.org/wiki/Forest_of_Compi%C3%A8gne
8. http://www.napoleon.org/en/magazine/museums/files/Musee_national_château_Compiegne-historic.asp
9. http://fr.wikipedia.org/wiki/Ch%C3%A2teau_de_Compi%C3%A8gne#L.27avenue_des_Beaux-Monts
10. http://www.reims-tourism.com/musee-de-la-reddition/commune/tabid/15267/offreid/cb2de5af-14c9-4cec-bd29-24db48aae3ee/museum.aspx
11. http://www.experienceloire.com/amboise-château.htm
12. http://www.fragonard.com/parfums_grasse/GB/fragonard/grasse/
13. http://www.fragonard.com/parfums_grasse/GB/fragonard/perfume_making_techniques/perfume_making_techniques/the_absorption.cfm
14. http://en.wikipedia.org/wiki/Arles_Amphitheatre
15. http://whc.unesco.org/en/list/164
16. http://www.winespectator.com/drvinny/show/id/5045
17. http://www.wallafaces.com/wine-grapes-vs-table-grapes-comparison/
18. http://www.livescience.com/27534-richard-lionheart-heart-mummified.html
19. http://en.wikipedia.org/wiki/Church_of_St_Joan_of_Arc

# INDEX